Robert E. Strahorn

**The Resources and Attractions of Idaho**

facts on farming, stock-raising, mining, lumbering, and other industries, and notes

on climate, scenery, game, fish, and health and pleasure resorts

.

Robert E. Strahorn

**The Resources and Attractions of Idaho**
*facts on farming, stock-raising, mining, lumbering, and other industries, and notes on
climate, scenery, game, fish, and health and pleasure resorts*

ISBN/EAN: 9783337844776

Printed in Europe, USA, Canada, Australia, Japan

Cover: Foto ©Andreas Hilbeck / pixelio.de

More available books at **www.hansebooks.com**

# IDAHO

## A Complete and Comprehensive Description

OF THE

# AGRICULTURAL,

# STOCK RAISING AND

# MINERAL RESOURCES

OF IDAHO.

## Also Statistics in regard to its Climate, etc.,

Compiled from the Latest Reports of 1891.

Presented with the Compliments of the

## PASSENGER DEPARTMENT,

UNION PACIFIC

THE OVERLAND ROUTE

FIFTH EDITION
Revised and Enlarged

WOODWARD & TIERNAN PRINTING CO
ST. LOUIS.

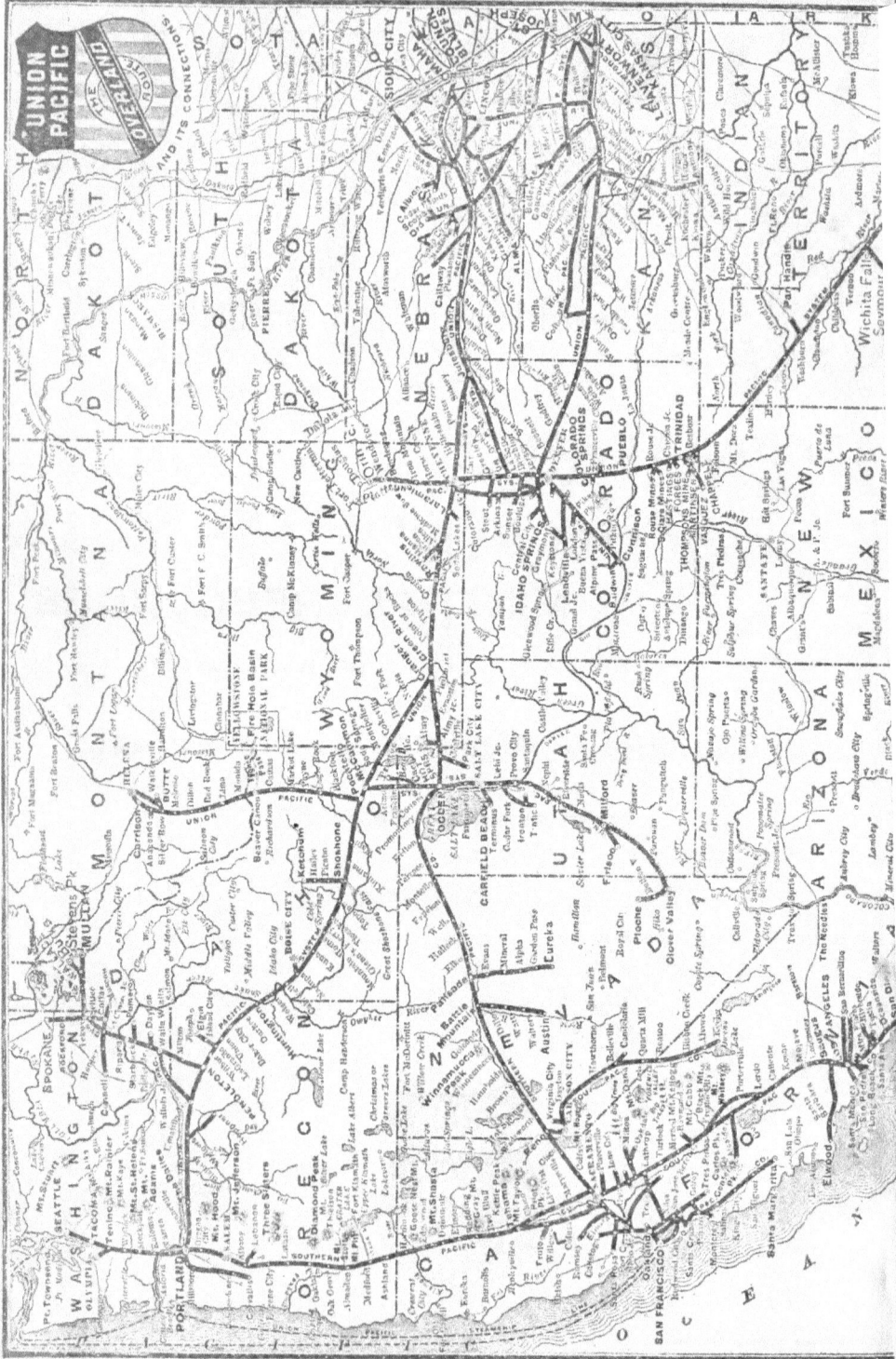

—THE—

# RESOURCES AND ATTRACTIONS

—OF ·

# IDAHO

FACTS ON FARMING, STOCK-RAISING, MINING, LUMBERING, AND OTHER
INDUSTRIES, AND NOTES ON CLIMATE, SCENERY, GAME, FISH,
AND HEALTH AND PLEASURE RESORTS.

WITH THE COMPLIMENTS OF THE

## PASSENGER DEPARTMENT.

FIFTH EDITION.

ST. LOUIS.
WOODWARD & TIERNAN PRINTING CO., 309-319 NORTH THIRD STREET.
1892.

A COMPLETE AND
COMPREHENSIVE DESCRIPTION
OF THE AGRICULTURAL, STOCK-RAISING
AND MINERAL RESOURCES OF IDAHO; ALSO STATISTICS
IN REGARD TO ITS CLIMATE, ETC.,
COMPILED FROM THE LATEST
REPORTS OF 1891.

———

*FIFTH EDITION.*

———

OMAHA, MARCH 1, 1892.

———

# AN OUTLINE.

Idaho is imperial in extent. Its area is greater than that of New York, New Jersey, Massachusetts, and New Hampshire combined.

Its climate is proved by official reports of leading nations to be the healthiest in the world.

Its arable belts enjoy the influence of the warm currents of the Pacific, and are of grand proportions, and unexcelled for productiveness.

Its mineral fields are among the largest in the world, and they have produced, and are now producing, the richest ores known in the history of mining.

It contains a diversity of other resources not surpassed by any region of similar extent in our Union.

It is now rendered easily accessible by the Union Pacific Railway and its branches, and possesses water communications with the Pacific Ocean. These avenues insure the producer every facility for transportation, and the settler of the immediate future a very rapid increase in the value of his possessions, whatever they may be.

With such a vast extent of public domain unoccupied, and presenting opportunities no more to be enjoyed in the East or "Middle West," for acquiring homes and wealth, Idaho also possesses many of the religious, educational and social advantages of those localities.

# CONTENTS.

(5)

# IDAHO.

## LOCATION, AREA, AND PHYSICAL FEATURES.

Idaho is an Indian word, which, being translated, means "Gem of the Mountains." The first white man who set foot upon the soil of Idaho was Captain Lewis, with a detachment of Lewis and Clark's exploring expedition. Captain Lewis crossed the main range of the Rocky Mountains from Horse Plains, now known as Horse Prairie, in Beaverhead county, Montana, to the Lemhi, a tributary of Salmon River, on the 12th day of August, 1805. Five years later the Missouri Fur Company established a trading post on Snake River, but soon after abandoned it. In 1811, Wilson P. Hunt, with sixty men of the Pacific Fur Company, passed through Idaho to the Pacific coast. In 1834, Captain Bonneville, with his company of nearly one hundred men, spent part of the season in Eastern Idaho, exploring the head waters of the Snake and Salmon rivers. In the same year a party of traders and trappers, commanded by Nathaniel I. Wythe, established Fort Hall as a trading post, near Snake River, and on the present Fort Hall Indian Reservation.

In 1860 gold in paying quantities was discovered in Idaho by a party of prospectors, commanded by Capt. James Pierce, from Walla Walla Valley, Washington. The first locations were on Oro Fino creek, a tributary of the Clearwater. Other valuable discoveries followed in rapid succession. The first permanent settlement was made at Mount Idaho, the present county seat of Idaho county, May, 1861.

Idaho was created a Territory by act of Congress, March 3, 1863, from parts of Dakota, Nebraska and Washington Territories. Originally it embraced within its boundaries about 325,000 square miles. By the creation of the Territories of Montana and Wyoming, under the act of Congress May 25, 1868, Idaho was finally reduced to 86,294 square miles, or 55,228,160 acres. It extends from the British Possessions on the north to Utah and Nevada on the south; from Montana and Wyoming on the east to Oregon and Washington on the west; having a length from north to south of about 410 miles, and a width from east to west varying from 44 to 306½ miles. Idaho was admitted as a State into the Union July 3, 1890.

There are 18,400,000 acres classed as mountainous, 15,000,000 acres agricultural lands, 7,000,000 acres of forests, 25,000,000 acres grazing lands, and some 600,000 acres lakes. Its vast mineral belts are included in the mountain area, as are also most of its forests.

Stretching along its eastern edge, and separating Idaho from Montana and Wyoming, are the rugged mountains of the Bitter Root, Rocky and

Wahsatch ranges, the Bitter Root occupying the northern, the Rocky the central, and the Wahsatch the southern links in this boundary. The "spurs" of these ranges, especially of the Wahsatch, extend well over into Idaho, and they contain some of the State's best mineral belts. Their highest peaks reach altitudes ranging from 9,000 to 13,000 feet. On the south and southwest are the Owyhee Mountains, which form an important link in the great divide between the waters of the Columbia and those of the Humboldt. The Sawtooth, Salmon River, Wood River, and Boise are among the prominent mountain ranges in Central Idaho. On the west are the Blue Mountains of Oregon and Washington. Idaho is, therefore, practically mountain-locked, although from the south, southeast and west there are numerous depressions through which railway and wagon roads find easy, natural access. The interior of the State is a vast plateau, varying in altitude from 600 feet above the sea in its lowest valleys, to 10,000 on the tops of its highest peaks. The average elevation is from 2,000 to 3,000 feet less than that of Wyoming, Utah, Nevada or Colorado. Its numerous mountain ranges run in a variety of directions, the trend of the principal ones, however, being southeast to northwest. In these interior ranges are the mineral belts which first attracted general attention to the then Territory.

Alternating and nestling among the mountain ranges are many valleys, large and small, affording in the aggregate a vast area of agricultural lands not exceeded in fertility by any in the world. Through these meander a river system well worthy of the extended notice which is given in succeeding pages. The arable portions of the valleys lie from 600 to 6,000 feet above the sea, and they range in size from one to twenty miles in width, and from twenty to one hundred miles in length.

Traversing Southern Idaho is the extensive volcanic belt on the basin of Snake River. This basin stretches far into neighboring States, being 800 miles in length. In Idaho it averages about fifty miles in width. Some of the best valleys traverse it, but it is more noteworthy as the great winter grazing region of this and adjacent States. Its nutritious herbs and grasses fatten thousands of cattle and sheep annually.

## CLIMATOLOGY AND HEALTH.

The State of Idaho is in the same latitude as France, Switzerland, portions of Italy, Spain and Portugal. It is subject to oceanic influences very similar to those countries, and necessarily has a somewhat similar climate. All this region is near enough to the Pacific Ocean to be noticeably affected by its currents. By reference to any map whereon these ocean currents are shown, it will be seen that the great Japan current (Kuro Siwa)—that mighty stream of warm water—bears directly against the western shores of America. The temperature of the winds blowing over it is, of course, affected by its heat, and they carry their modifying influences inland hundreds of miles, even extending their genial influences upon the climate of Montana. Cast your eye over a climatic map exhibiting the extreme northern line of wheat production, for instance, and you will find that, while on the eastern shore it touches near the mouth of the St. Lawrence at latitude 50°, it runs in the northwest nearly 1,000 miles north of the most nor therly part of Idaho.

The average or mean annual temperature at Lewiston, in Northern Idaho, is 56°, a milder showing by five degrees than is made by Ohio, milder by ten degrees than Iowa, and milder by twelve degrees than Maine and New Hampshire. Boise City, in Western Central Idaho, with a much greater altitude than Lewiston, has an average temperature of 51°, the same as Ohio, and four degrees warmer than Connecticut. The rain and snow fall at Lewiston is about twenty-four inches; at Boise City about half that amount. At Boise City the lowest record during seven consecutive winters was 12° below zero in January, and the highest 108° in July. The United States signal officer, reports that mercury sank below zero only four times during one period of five years. The coldest weather recorded in twenty years was the exceptional January, 1888, when mercury sank to 27° below zero. The prevailing winds are south-southwest, averaging twelve miles an hour, and never exceeding thirty.

While Boise City is a fair representative, in the matter of climate, of the various agricultural sections, it should be borne in mind that the much more elevated mining districts have winters as harsh, in most ways, as any of the regions of the Allegheny or Blue Ridge Mountains. Our best authorities on climatology, however, agree that in the dry, rarefied atmosphere of Idaho, and the mountainous regions adjoining on the east, there is a difference of about twenty degrees in the intensity of the heat or cold in favor of those regions, when compared with the same temperature in the raw and humid atmosphere of the Atlantic Coast region. In other words, a temperature of 105° in Idaho is only equal in its effects upon the system to one of 85° at Boston or New York; or the extreme cold temperature of Boise City of 12° below zero, is as easily endured as that of 8° above at any point in the Eastern States. Referring to this peculiarity of the Idaho climate, Hon E. A. Stevenson, late Governor of the Territory, says:—

"The lowest temperature in the history of the Boise Signal Station was —27.8°, on January 16, 1888. At this time the signal officer regularly walked from his office to his residence and back without an overcoat, and he noticed many other men on the streets without overcoats. Such habits are very possible in the exceptionally fine climate of Idaho. This occurred during the twenty days when a thousand persons froze to death between the Rocky Mountains and the Mississippi River. Rarely ever does the temperature fall to zero. This highly oxygenated atmosphere is specially adapted to the cure of catarrh, consumption, and many diseases in which a cure depends upon a purification of the blood. At this date, October 9th, there has been no frost. The most tender vines and flowers are as vigorous and fresh as in the spring.".

Sunstroke and hydrophobia are never known in Idaho, and although open-air work is carried on every day in winter, and an important proportion of the population live among the mines and on the stock ranges, in the rudest kind of shelter, the year round, a case of severe freezing as a result of such exposure is never heard of. The sky is usually free from clouds, and sunshiny days are the rule. Idaho averages 260 days of perfect sunshine per

year, and 300 *fair days*, as against 191 fair days in Boston, and 170 at Buf-
falo and Chicago.   Of 600 cyclones recently reported by the United States
Signal Service as occurring during a long series of years, *not one was
reported in Idaho.*   Floods or other storms destructive of life and property
are almost unknown in the history of this region.   During harvest time
there is rarely any rainfall; in fact, such a catastrophe as loss of crops from
drouth or flood would be considered phenomenal.   The absence of showers is
not felt, because of the beneficial distribution of lands and streams suitable for
irrigation.   There is rarely enough snow for sleighing in the valleys,
although it is abundant in the mountains.

The influence of climate upon agriculture, stock-raising, or mere personal comfort is very important, but its effect upon the health is paramount
to every other consideration.   Statistics prove Idaho *the healthiest country
in the world.*   A careful study of the official reports which follow is better
than the reading of volumes of glittering generalities so often put forth in
the interest of the many noted health resorts.   The figures prove beyond
question the truth of the above claim as to Idaho's healthfulness.

According to the mortality statistics, taken in connection with our
National census, the death rate in Idaho is *less than in any other State or
Territory*, as will be seen from the following table, giving the exact figures
of the census.   The percentage of deaths was as follows:—

| | | | |
|---|---|---|---|
| Idaho.... | 0.33 | District of Columbia | 1.53 |
| Alabama. | 1.08 | Florida | 1.21 |
| Arizona | 2.61 | Georgia | 1.15 |
| Arkansas | 1.26 | Illinois | 1.33 |
| California | 1.61 | Indiana. | 1.03 |
| Colorado | 0.94 | Iowa | 0 81 |
| Connecticut | 1.26 | Kansas | 1.25 |
| Dakota | 0.71 | Kentucky | 1.09 |
| Delaware | 1.25 | North Carolina | 0 98 |
| Louisiana | 2.00 | Ohio | 1.11 |
| Maine | 1.23 | Oregon | 0.69 |
| Maryland | 1.24 | Pennsylvania | 1.49 |
| Massachusetts | 1.77 | Rhode Island | 1 20 |
| Michigan | 0.94 | South Carolina. | 1.05 |
| Minnesota | 0.80 | Tennessee | 1.13 |
| Mississippi | 1.11 | Texas | 1.37 |
| Missouri | 1.53 | Utah | 1.03 |
| Montana | 0.90 | Vermont | 1.07 |
| Nebraska | 0.81 | Virginia | 1.24 |
| Nevada | 1.45 | Washington | 0.93 |
| New Hampshire | 1.85 | West Virginia | 0.91 |
| New Jersey | 1.17 | Wisconsin | 0.94 |
| New Mexico | 1.28 | Wyoming | 0.81 |
| New York | 1.58 | | |

It will be observed that the mortality of California—the praises of whose
climate are carolled in all civilized tongues—is nearly five times greater
than that of Idaho: Colorado, a summer land which is most deservedly the
resort of tens of thousands of health seekers annually, exhibits a mortality
nearly three times as great as that of Idaho, while Florida, ''where 'tis
springtime all the year.''and where our best physicians of all Eastern States
unite in directing multitudes of patients, makes a showing about three times
less favorable than that of Idaho.

But it is sometimes insisted that the United States Army mortality
statistics are the more valuable, because the troops of the United States
Army are subjected to exactly the same conditions and surroundings, and

have the same habits everywhere, more nearly than any other class of people. Their food, clothing, medical attendance, and places of abode are nearly identically the same wherever they go; consequently, comparing the ratio of mortality among them in these different regions leads to a more correct estimate of the actual healthfulness of each region than could possibly be obtained in any other way.

According to official reports of the Surgeon-General of the United States Army, the percentage of deaths from disease to each 1,000 soldiers in the different military districts of the Union are as follows, the results having been the average of many years:—

| Localities. | Deaths each year from Disease. |
|---|---|
| Gulf States | 22.50 |
| Atlantic Coast States | 17 83 |
| Arizona | 12.11 |
| Pennsylvania and Michigan | 6.05 |
| New Mexico | 7.77 |
| Montana | 5.62 |
| California | 6.83 |
| Dakota | 4.76 |
| Wyoming | 4.71 |
| Idaho | 3.74 |

Or let us compare the prevalence of certain *diseases* in the different parts of the United States. In an equal number of the soldiers in the different departments during the years 1868 and 1869, the number of cases of sickness (not deaths) by malarial fever, stood nearly in the following proportion:—

| | |
|---|---|
| Department of the East | 30 |
| Department of the South | 60 |
| Department of the Lakes | 50 |
| New Mexico, Indian Territory, Kansas, Arkansas, and Missouri, over | 40 |
| Wyoming, Nebraska, and Utah | 20 |
| Montana, Dakota, and Minnesota, nearly | 10 |
| Department of the Columbia (Oregon, Washington, and Idaho) | 10 |
| Department of California | 20 |
| Department of Arizona | 160 |

Or compare the mortality, in the different sections, by the great destroyer of human life, consumption, and other respiratory diseases. There die annually in every 1,000 soldiers, by consumption, pneumonia, etc.:—

| | |
|---|---|
| In Florida, an average of | 2.75 |
| In Texas | 3 |
| In New Mexico and Arizona | 3.15 |
| In California, a little more than | 3 |
| In Idaho, only | 1.6 |

So that combining these two set of statistics, both in regard to the entire mortality, and also to the mortality by the principal diseases, we have Idaho shown to be the *very healthiest part of the United States.*

But we will go farther, and repeat that, so far as we have the vital statistics, to determine, there is *no climate in the world* that can compare with that of Idaho. Take Italy, the South of France, and Algiers, to which invalids are sent, both the civil and military statistics show a much higher mortality there than here. In presenting the following figures, as well as the preceding, perfect fairness has been observed. Particular years are taken, not at all because they favor a theory, but because they are obtainable and in form to be compared. The death rate per annum, by all dis-cases, in the Italian army, from 1860 to 1876, was about 11 in 1,000. Among the soldiers of the French army, stationed in the south of France, in 1872, it was 10 in 1,000. In the French army in Algiers, during the years 1863, 1864, 1866, and 1870, it was 14.50, while in Idaho, the death rate, from 1868 to 1881, was only 3.75 in 1,000 *by all diseases.*

Or let us compare the figures for the diseases of the respiratory organs, including consumption, pneumonia, etc., and we have among the soldiers in the South of France (including the health resorts of Nice, Mentone, etc.), for the year 1872, an average death rate, by these diseases, of 2.4 per 1,000 annually. In the French army in Algeria, during the years 1863, 1864, and 1866, it was, by these diseases, more than 3 in 1,000 annually; and in the Italian army during the years 1867, 1868, 1869, 1874, 1875, and 1876, the deaths by respiratory diseases, including consumption, etc., averaged nearly 4 in 1,000 annually, while in Idaho the mortality by these diseases, from 1870 to 1881, was *less than 1 in 1,000 annually.*

All this is confirmed in a remarkable manner by the records of the medical department of the British army from 1859 to 1879. These records show the sanitary condition of the British soldiers, the disease and deaths which occur in every military station in the British Dominions, and consequently represent the healthfulness or unhealthfulness of climate in portions of every quarter of the globe—Europe, Asia, Africa, North and South America, and Islands of Australia, New Zealand, and the East and West Indies—a mass of official, and certainly very valuable statistics.

From 1859 to 1879, at the British stations of Gibraltar, the Ionian Islands, and Malta, in the supposed sanitary zone of the Mediterranean, we find an average death rate, by all diseases, of about 7.5, 8.4, and 10.5, respectively, in each 1,000 troops per annum, and by respiratory diseases, including consumption, pneumonia, etc., of 2 in 1,000, being more than twice as great as in Idaho. In Australia we find a death rate from all diseases, of 12 in each 1,000 troops annually, and by respiratory diseases, of over 5 in 1,000. In New Zealand, of 8.75 by all diseases, and nearly 3 per 1,000 by respiratory diseases. Japan, China, and the East Indies are much worse, having a mortality of from 14 to 25 in 1,000 troops. In the West Indies it is, by all diseases, from 10 to 12 and 13 in 1,000, and by respiratory diseases, over 2 per annum. In England itself, the mortality is about 8 in 1,000 soldiers, by all diseases annually, and by respiratory diseases, over 3.5. In Canada it is between 6 and 7 per 1,000 by all diseases, and over 2 by respiratory diseases; while in British Columbia, lying immediately north of Idaho, and having a climate quite similar, the death rate per annum for the four and a half years the British troops were there, was a little over 3 in 1,000 (3.04) by all diseases, being almost exactly the same as among our own soldiers in Idaho, in the department of the Columbia, so similarly situated. Indeed, the British troops were stationed less than fifty miles from our boundary line.

Thus after making the circuit of the globe in search of health, we come back to find Idaho and the country adjacent to it—extending from the Rocky Mountains to the coast regions—the healthiest country, so far as we have any positive and reliable evidence, *in the world.*

With the possibility of living at any desired elevation above the sea level; with a rarefied, dry, pure atmosphere, with almost constantly bright, genial sunshine; with a light, dry soil, and with an abundance of pure water, fresh from mountain streams, or medicinal waters from numerous springs, is it any wonder that Idaho is *the healthiest region in the world?* Children born here are strong and sturdy, and diseases incident to childhood never assume a malignant form. Endemic and epidemic diseases are almost unknown. There are no low, swampy lands here, malaria cannot exist, and fever and ague have no foothold. Consumption that "dread disease which medicine never cured, riches never warded off, nor poverty could boast exemption from," which is the scourge and terror of New England and all other moist climates, is either here cured, or modified so as to prolong life for many years. The dryness, purity and antiseptic properties of the air have a tendency to counteract and reduce the excessive mucous collections, while its rarefaction makes necessary more frequent and deeper respirations, thus causing a wholesome expansion of the lungs. The bright, warm days are conducive to a cheerful and hopeful feeling, which is a great aid in overcoming the disease, while the cool nights are productive of sound, invigorating sleep. These influences are no less effective in rheumatism, asthma, bronchitis, liver complaint, dyspepsia, and many other diseases. In the various mineral springs, both hot and cold, with which the State abounds, the patient afflicted with scrofulous or glandular diseases finds veritable pools of Bethesda.

## RIVERS, WATER-COURSES, AND SPRINGS.

Of swift, noble rivers, Idaho has its scores. With the exception of a comparatively small portion of Southeastern Idaho, whose waters flow into the Basin of Great Salt Lake, the river system of Idaho is entirely tributary to the Valley of the great Columbia River. There are three important rivers in Idaho which empty directly into the Columbia, namely, the Spokane, Clark's Fork, and the Snake. Snake river meanders through the eastern, southern and western parts of the State for over 1,000 miles, and, next to Niagara, boasts the most imposing cataract on the Continent—the great Shoshone Falls. It rises among the most marvelous scenes of the Yellowstone National Park, within a few feet of the crystal founts from which springs that great tributary of the Mississippi—the Yellowstone, and within sight of the headwaters of that grand inlet of the Gulf of California—the Rio Colorado. Here, at its romantic start, the Snake is also only a day's ride from its twin torrent of the North, Clark's Fork, but soon sweeps southward 500 miles, as if to gather in the waters of wider and richer fields. Again, flowing majestically northward to mark the boundary between Idaho and Oregon, it unites, when within 400 miles of the Pacific, with the Clark's Fork system to form the Columbia. It will lead the reader toward a true appreciation of the wondrous volume of the Snake River, when he is informed that soundings of the deep, blue stream in Eastern Idaho, near the crossing of the Utah Northern Railway, fail to discover bottom at 240 feet.

The Salmon, Boise, Payette, Weiser, and Wood Rivers drain Central and Southern Idaho, flowing into the Snake River from the north. The Clearwater, Clark's Fork, Cœur d'Alene, St. Joseph, and Kootenai are all great rivers in Northern Idaho. The Snake River is navigable for 300 miles above its junction with Clark's Fork, and for 200 miles in the heart of Idaho, 1,000 miles from the sea, as well as for shorter stretches in other localities. The Clearwater also affords a considerable distance of navigable waters.

Clark's Fork, Cœur d'Alene, and St. Joseph Rivers are each navigable, and larger than the Ohio at Pittsburg. The Salmon, Clearwater, Kootenai, and Payette are larger and compare favorably in picturesqueness with the Susquehanna, the Juniata or Schuylkill, which are recognized as the noblest and most beautiful streams of the Alleghanies or Blue Ridge. All of these and hundreds of minor streams are swift, with clear currents, and are full of trout, salmon, and other species of fresh-water fish. They furnish power illimitable in extent and easily utilized, and a never-failing supply of water for irrigation and domestic purposes. They are also of incalculable value for floating forest products from the mountains to consumers in the valleys. Some of the streams, of which Big and Little Lost Rivers are notable examples, apparently sink into the sage-brush plains, but in reality doubtless have subterranean outlets underneath the lava into Snake or some of its tributaries.

Idaho possesses many beautiful and valuable springs, aside from the mineral springs which are treated under the heading "Health and Pleasure Resorts." The cold springs, large and small, with water clear as crystal and often almost ice-cold, are the sources of many of the smaller streams, In the vicinity of Hailey, all about Caldwell, and in every portion of the State, in fact, near the foot-hills and in the mountain valleys, are these beautiful founts. They are of particular value to various cities and to dairymen and farmers At Hailey, Bellevue, and Boise City, for example, the city water-works are supplied by large springs of pure, cold water, located in the hills so high above as to afford an ample pressure for domestic and fire purposes. The settler often depends on large springs for irrigation and for water for his stock, as well as for their cooling influence in the milk house and dairy. Some springs of immense volumes—flowing a river of water—burst from the palisades of Snake River, south of Mountain Home, and, falling with terrific force several hundred feet into the deep torrent below, are among the prominent wonders and scenic attractions of Idaho.

## TIMBER.

The forest area is 7,000,000 acres, much of it being included in the mountain region already described. Throughout the central, northern, and eastern parts of Idaho the woodlands possess a heavier growth than in a majority of the timbered States east of the Rocky Mountains, while in the remaining sections the timber supply is equal to that of most of our prairie States. There are various varieties of fir, white, red, and black spruce, scrub oak, yellow and white pine, mountain mahogany, juniper, tamarack, birch, cottonwood, alder, and willow.

From careful estimates received from eighteen different parts of the State, from data furnished by Messrs. Williams and Paul, census statisticians, and from Dr. Brewster's "Forests of America," it is safe to give the approximate area of these woodlands as follows: Ten thousand square miles contain over 500 acres of timber to the square mile; 12,000 square miles, from 360 to 500 acres; 5,000 square miles, from 240 to 360 acres; 15,000 square miles, from 120 to 240 acres; 13,500 square miles, from 10 to 120 acres.

The railroad travelers crossing Eastern and Southern Idaho, after traversing the vast extent of sage-brush plains, would hardly imagine that within the State there are immense forests of timber, in many places so thick as to exclude the light of the sun. In Boise, Lemhi, Custer, and Alturas counties are extensive forests. The upper waters of the Boise River, and its tributaries, including the South Fork, are heavily timbered. The amount of merchantable timber in that section is estimated at from 80,000,000 to 90,000,000 feet, exclusive of the South Fork, which is claimed to be more heavily timbered than either of the other tributaries. These forests extend thirty or forty miles into the mountains, and consist of white pine, fir, and cottonwood in abundance. The tributaries of the Upper Salmon also abound with the same kind of timber. On Salmon and Craig's Mountains, in Idaho county, an extensive body of excellent timber is found, reaching from the Snake River, near the mouth of the Salmon River, to and across the north fork of the Clearwater, some sixty miles. It is estimated that this belt is from five to ten miles in width, and consists of white and yellow pine, red and yellow fir, and white cedar. This timber is of large growth, and valuable for lumbering purposes. Spruce and tamarack are found on the Lolo Creek, a tributary of the Clearwater. Yew trees, a foot in diameter, are found on the upper part of the Clearwater. White pine logs, five feet in diameter, and 100 feet in length, without a knot, have been rafted down the Clearwater, furnishing the finest quality of lumber for finishing purposes.

The greatest timber regions are in Shoshone and Kootenai counties, in extreme North Idaho. The Pend d'Oreille forests extend in all directions from the lake, covering an area over a hundred miles square. Gigantic monarchs of the forest lift their heads aloft at a height of over 200 feet, bull pine, white pine, tamarack, and fir predominating, while cedar attains marvelous height and thickness. From many of the trees the Spanish moss hangs in long graceful festoons, adding a pleasing variety to the otherwise sombre scene. "This superb forest of the Pen d'Oreille," observes a writer in the *Century Magazine*, "is a vast lumber preserve for future generations. The pineries of Michigan and Minnesota look like open parks compared with it. Nowhere else in the United States, save on the western slopes of the western mountains in Washington, can be found such a prodigious amount of timber to the acre."

The Payette forests, whose product finds ready market along the Oregon Short Line Railway, are among the finest in Idaho. These are largely drawn upon for building, fencing, and other improvements all over South-

ern Idaho.  All forest products are as cheap to the settler in Idaho as they
are to the farmer in the Mississippi Valley.

## THE SOIL OF IDAHO.

In such a vast area as is included within Idaho's boundary, traversed by
mountain ranges formed of rocks of all kinds and ages, there is necessarily
a great variety of soil.  For the sake of convenience, her soils have been
divided into four classes. as follows:—

1. Valley soil, which cannot be excelled in any other State or Territory
in the Union.  It contains, indeed, the aggregated and condensed richness
of the vast areas of vegetable growth that have been accumulating for ages
on the sides of the mountains skirting the valleys.  An analysis of this soil
shows it to be pre-eminently rich in all the mineral and vegetable elements
necessary to the growth of all cereals, vegetables, fruits, etc., usually grown
within the limits of the State.  It is of good depth, is invariably found
to superimpose a gravelly soil, and is so inclined that perfect drainage can
be readily and effectively had.

2. Plain and plateau soil, which contains all the elements for the successful growths of all the cereals, containing a great amount of vegetable mold.
Not less than three-fourths of all the arable lands of Idaho are included in
this class.

3. Mountain soil.  This soil is exceedingly rich, especially in the wooded
sections, where it is black, deep, and full of vegetable mold.  All narrow
valleys and parks in the mountains possess this soil.

4. Alkali soil.  This soil is of limited extent, producing greasewood and
salt grass, which cattle eat readily, particularly the young shoots.  The
cause of alkaline soils is now generally well understood.  The rain which
falls during the wet season penetrates deeply into the earth, where it gradually takes up such soluble salts as it encounters there, and as it has accu-
mulated beneath, has gradually risen by percolation through the interstices of
the unconsolidated materials of the soil, bringing with it whatever soluble
salts it may have taken into solution during its sojourn beneath the surface.
"There is no difficulty, however," says Capt. C. E. Dutton, of the United
States Geological Survey, "in removing any quantity of these readily soluble salts from the soil, providing the leaching process be continued long
enough; and it is usually found that lands which were originally highly
alkaline, become, when reclaimed from their alkalinity, among the most
fertile."

It is a well established fact that irrigation has the effect of enriching any
of these classes of soils.  During the irrigating season the streams are
generally high and turbid, carrying in solution large quantities of vegetable
mold, which spread very evenly by the process of irrigation, acts not unlike
a top dressing of manure, and this is repeated annually.

Gen'l Carter, of Boise City, late Surveyor-General of Idaho, says: "Open
a trench of furrow through a newly-plowed field, and let that muddy water
through it; at first it will soak through its banks, and by percolating wet
the earth on each side for a distance of perhaps two feet; by that time there

will be a lining of fine silt to the trench, and no water will go through it. You can not irrigate by percolation with this water, and you need fear no seepage from your ditches or canals. There will be a little in the beginning, but it will not last. We have to irrigate here by letting the water over the surface in a sheet, or better, little drills, such as are formed by a harrow, and the result is that we get a layer of fine silt over all the land, which is the best fertilizer we can have. Our land grows richer by cropping, instead of poorer."

## DIVERSITY OF IDAHO AGRICULTURE.

There are 12,000,000 to 15,000,000 acres in the valleys and uplands of Idaho, lying at an elevation of less than 5,000 feet, which can be irrigated and made lavishly productive. We have already described the soils of these arable lands, and from the climatic facts also given, the reader will not require an elaborate argument to be satisfied that all the cereals and vegetables which can be raised north of the cotton-growing line in the Atlantic States flourish in the greatest perfection here, and that apples, pears, plums, peaches, grapes, nectarines, apricots, and many of the smaller fruits of the finest quality are almost as regularly produced as corn in the Missouri bottoms. Even tobacco and cotton have been grown in the lower valleys, experiments with the latter in 1887, especially, having been very satisfactory. There has been no general failure of crops in the Boise Valley in the past seventeen years.

IRRIGATION.—Irrigation is the process of conducting water from its natural channels by means of canals and ditches, so as to overflow the lower lands for farming purposes. To those only familiar with the very slight fall of streams of the Middle States, irrigation is apt to appear impracticable, but in the valleys and on the plains of the mountainous regions of the West, the velocity of the streams is so great, and the fall so rapid, that it is perfectly feasible.

In the southern half of Idaho irrigation is generally necessary to insure a ripening of crops. This the Idaho farmer considers an advantage. He is entirely free from solicitude in regard to drouth or flood while his grain is ripening, and is sure of pleasant weather during harvest time. Irrigation enables him to keep his pastures green in autumn, or start them early in the spring; it enables him to produce heavier crops and to secure a larger growth of fruit trees, shrubbery, etc., in one season than can be obtained by any unaided process of nature. The same stream that beautifies and fertilizes his soil, can be led by his door and be made to furnish power for his churn, grindstone, saw, fanning mill, etc. Better than all these, it carries to his land just such qualities of mineral and gaseous matter as is needed to keep it productive for years. In New Mexico, lands have been regularly cultivated in this way, without any other fertilizer, for 200 years. In the Valley of the Nile it has been the principal fertilizer on lands cultivated continuously for over 3,000 years.

COST OF IRRIGATION.—The expense of irrigating Idaho lands each season ranges from 50 cents to $1.25 per acre. To dig the ditches originally and clear the sage-brush from Idaho farms is a much less expense than improving and cultivating lands in the East possessing a light growth of timber, while the annual cost of irrigating, above ordinary farming in the Eastern States, is more than covered by the acknowledged greater yield and superior quality of the grain produced. One man can irrigate eighty acres of cereals or forty acres of corn or potatoes, or twenty acres of garden stuff. If done by the farmer himself, it does not interfere with the regular work of the farm, coming as it does at a time when even Eastern farmers have but little to do save wait upon the weather prophet and sigh for rain that does not come. Streams possessing an abundance of water the year round, and having a rapid descent, are almost everywhere available. Canal companies lease water from 75 cents to $1.25 per acre per year, or they will sell perpetual water rights, subject to a small annual assessment for canal repairs, at from $6 to $8 per acre. In many localities a community of farmers unite and construct their own canals.

However, the new-comer who prefers such conditions as surrounded him in the East, will in Northern Idaho find vast areas of unclaimed territory, where the rainfall is ample to insure the growth of all crops. This also applies in some mountain valleys of Southern and Central Idaho as well as to large areas of bottom-lands along various streams.

WHEAT.—Wheat of all varieties is successfully grown at all altitudes and on all soils in the arable portion of Idaho. It yields an average of thirty bushels per acre. Both spring and fall wheat are grown, but the former predominates, as there is so little snow in the lower valleys to shelter the tender sprouts of fall-sown grain. The quality of Idaho wheat cannot be excelled in the world, the berry being plump, hard and bright, and, on account of the unfailing clear weather, is rarely affected by any of the evils common in rainy regions.

BARLEY.—The above, relating to wheat, is in a general way applicable to barley, but the yield averages forty bushels per acre. The quality is such that brewers of Chicago and Milwaukee eagerly purchase it at a rate which insures a good profit.

OATS.—Oats grow anywhere and yield fifty-five to seventy-five bushels per acre. They are very heavy, generally weighing forty-five pounds to the bushel.

RYE.—Rye of the finest quality is successfully grown in all localities. It is sown both in the spring and fall, and is much used for pasturage.

FLAX.—The first crop of flax was sown in North Idaho, near Lewiston, in 1878, and yielded from twenty to twenty-five bushels to the acre. Since then the cultivation of flax has become quite general in Northern Idaho. Near Genessee, at M. Hensen's ranch, thirty-two bushels are raised to the acre. It is worth from $1.25 to $1.65 per bushel.

CORN.—Owing to the cool nights, Idaho is not generally considered a first-class corn producing region; but good crops of a superior quality are raised in all the lower districts, such as Boise Valley, Payette Valley, Weiser Valley, etc. Early Dent and flint are the principal varieties, although at the fair of the Caldwell Fair Association, held at Caldwell, in November, 1887, one exhibitor had sixteen varieties of field corn, besides several varieties of sweet and pop corn. Stalks fifteen feet high, with two or three well-filled ears to the stalk, were exhibited by others.

BROOM CORN AND SORGHUM are successfully produced in various localities, and the raw material is worked up at a handsome profit. Idaho sorghum is especially rich in the best juices entering into the composition of syrups and sugar.

TOBACCO AND SWEET POTATOES, of several, varieties, flourish in the milder belts of Southern Idaho.

GRASSES.—The natural grasses abound, both on the mountain-side and in valley, hence but little attention has been paid to the cultivated varieties. But blue grass, orchard grass, red top, timothy, alfalfa, and clover, wherever sown, have grown prolifically, and they are hardy in growth, clover and alfalfa, especially, yielding three and four crops of from one to three tons to each, per acre, in one season. Timothy and clover have been grown together, producing grass knee high, and making splendid food for horses and cattle.

Alfalfa is the king of Idaho grasses, its yield in many cases being almost incredible, and its fattening properties approaching nearer to those of grain than any other grass.

VEGETABLES.—Potatoes yield abundantly, averaging over 200 bushels to the acre, equal to the finest grown in Utah, varying in price from $1 to $3 per 100 pounds, according to the season. When they are well watered they are of large size, white, mealy, and delicious. Many thousand car-loads of potatoes were shipped from Idaho points over the Union Pacific Railway in 1887, 1888, 1889 and 1890 to Eastern markets, where they are in great demand. All kinds of garden vegetables, such as beets, peas, squashes, beans, tomatoes, cucumbers, rhubarb, onions, etc., are successfully cultivated. The crop is enormous, the quality good, and a profitable market is readily found for all that is not needed at home. Nearly every farmer has his garden well stocked with all kinds of vegetables. Cabbages average twelve pounds to the head, and sweet corn, lettuce, melons, radishes, egg-plant, etc., are noticeably thrifty and superior. The market is a consideration not to be overlooked by intending settlers, since abundant crops would be of little value if no market at remunerative rates was to be had close at home, or within easy reach by rail.

## AGRICULTURAL DEVELOPMENT OF THE STATE.

Governor Shoup, in his report for 1889, says:—

" It is exceedingly difficult to estimate the acreage of agricultural lands in Idaho. There are vast areas not yet officially explored. Prospectors seeking only the precious minerals have taken no note of the value of the land for the purposes of food production, and the most intelligent observation is yet inconclusive unless at the same time the quantity and availability of the water-supply is taken into the account. Conservative estimates give us 13,000,000 acres of agricultural lands. Others place the amount at 20,000,000. I think it safe to estimate it at 15,000,000 to 16,000,000 acres. Our industrious pioneers have already brought under cultivation about 4 per cent, or 600,000 acres, expending $2,000,000 in irrigating canals alone.

"The altitude of the land governs to a large extent the character of its productions. The valleys of Bear Lake, Lemhi, and Custer counties are profitably cultivated at an elevation of 6,000 feet above tide-water, and at 5,000 feet, oats, wheat, potatoes, turnips, etc., are raised abundantly  Timothy and a few hardy grasses flourish at these altitudes. At 4,000 to 4,500 feet all kinds of grain and vegetables are profitable, except a few tender garden products. In some localities fruit is grown successfully at 4,000 to 4,300 feet, and berries are abundant at 4,500. The Boise Valley, so prolific of all kinds of fruit, is 2,800 feet above the ocean, while the valleys of the Clearwater and Snake Rivers, near Lewiston in the northwest, with an altitude of but 680 feet, revel in tropical vegetation. Thus the Territory of Idaho, in addition to its invaluable mineral wealth, possesses a share of the best climatic influences of every portion of the Union.

"The soil in the valleys and on the plateaus, in the eastern and southern parts of the Territory, is composed of vegetable matter mixed with mineral, and in some localities with sand and clay. On this class of soil sage-brush grows extensively.

"In the northwestern counties, dark loam of great depth prevails. In the gulches and near the mountains, this soil is mixed with decayed rock. Alkali soil is limited to narrow strips, in widely separated localities, and rarely interferes with agriculture.

"The yield of all kinds of cereals, when land is irrigated, is most gratifying and is not surpassed by any State or Territory. The same can be said of all kinds of vegetables, while in many parts of the Territory tender vines produce abundantly.

"Idaho fruits can not be excelled in quality or flavor. Apples, pears, peaches, plums, prunes, apricots, grapes and all small fruits and berries are raised in great abundance. Huckleberries, gooseberries, and wild cherries grow wild in profusion on the mountain-sides and foot-hills. The camas, which gives a name to several prairies in the Territory is found in all sections. It is a bulb which is prized highly by the Indians for food."

## GROWTH OF THE STATE.

The population in 1890, of Idaho, by counties, was as follows, according to the United States census returns:

| COUNTIES. | Population. | COUNTIES. | Population. |
|---|---|---|---|
| Ada | 8,284 | Latah | 9,422 |
| Alturas | 2,626 | Lemhi | 1,916 |
| Bear Lake | 6,061 | Logan | 5,151 |
| Bingham | 13,492 | Nez Perces | 2,594 |
| Boise | 3,271 | Oneida | 6,827 |
| Cassia | 3,135 | Owyhee | 2,071 |
| Custer | 2,169 | Shoshone | 5,257 |
| Elmore | 1,876 | Washington | 3,828 |
| Idaho | 2,965 | Indians and Soldiers | 5,551 |
| Kootenai | 40,531 | Total | 90,549 |

Governor Shoup in his report for 1890 to the Secretary of the Interior, says:

"In my report for 1889 I estimated the population of the Territory to be 113,777. This estimate was reached through county assessors and from correspondence with intelligent and well-informed citizens in the several counties. In my last report I stated that—

"Mining being one of the principal industries, we find men in small parties engaged in working placer mines in distant and secluded sections, several miles distant from other mining camps. Again, we find men on the mountain slopes, and in some instances near the summit of our most lofty mountains, engaged in opening and developing quartz mines, which carry gold, silver, and other valuable metals. A considerable number of men are constantly employed in prospecting for mines. Small settlements are found in nearly all the mountain valleys. Settlements on the plains and in the lower valleys cover so large an area of country, that it is difficult to obtain a correct estimate of population among them."

"I had hoped that through the census enumerators we would be able to reach all isolated camps and settlements. In this I am disappointed. I have information that leads to the belief that thousands of our people were not enumerated. Advice from authentic sources is conclusive that many of our mines were not visited by the enumerators.

"Several large districts occupied by men engaged in prospecting for and in developing mines were overlooked or neglected. If the governors of States and Territories were confided·in and permitted to consult freely with enumerators, the census taking would be much more accurate and satisfactory. I am confident that the population of Idaho, if correctly enumerated, would be as large as estimated in my previous report. As an evidence of omissions, Boise City is reported to have a population of 2,982. The Boise City Board of Trade, knowing this to be erroneous, have, since the enumeration was made public, taken the census of the city and report 3,922 population. It is more than probable that persons were enumerated by the Board of Trade who were not in the city on June 1, but there could not have been any such difference as shown by the above figures. I have similar complaints from all parts of the State."

The Legislature at its thirteenth session passed a registry law, making it obligatory upon all voters to register, and requiring the voter to take a rigid test oath, which reads as follows:

You do solemnly swear (or affirm) that you are a male citizen of the United States over the age of twenty-one years; that you have actually resided in this Territory for four months last past and in this county thirty days; that you are not a bigamist or polygamist; that you are not a member of any order, organization, or association which teaches, advises, counsels, or encourages its members, devotees, or any other person to commit the crime of bigamy or polygamy, or any other crime defined by law, as a duty arising or resulting from membership in such order, organization, or association, or which practices bigamy or polygamy, or plural, or celestial marriage as a doctrinal rite of such organization; that you do not, either publicly or privately, or in any manner whatever, teach, advise, or encourage any person to commit the crime of bigamy or polygamy, or any other crime defined by law, either as a religious duty or otherwise; that you regard the Constitution of the United States and the laws thereof, and of this Territory, as interpreted by the courts, as the supreme law of the land, the teachings of any order, organization, or association to the contrary notwithstanding, and that you have not previously voted at this election; so help you God.

It is estimated that there are 25,000 Mormons in Idaho, and as polygamy is part of the doctrine taught by the Mormon Church, but few of their order took the oath. It is estimated that between 3,000 and 4,000 Mormon voters remained away from the polls.

## ANNUAL ASSESSMENT OF REAL AND PERSONAL PROPERTY FOR THE FISCAL YEAR 1890.

| COUNTIES. | Valuation. | COUNTIES. | Valuation. |
|---|---|---|---|
| Ada | $3,656,999 | Latah | $2,771,143 |
| Alturas | 645,802 | Lemhi | 671,000 |
| Bear Lake | 913,915 | Logan | 1,790,928 |
| Bingham | 3,177,658 | Nez Perces | 1,079,850 |
| Boise | 684,381 | Oneida | 1,086,990 |
| Cassia | 672,613 | Owyhee | 824,116 |
| Custer | 723,670 | Shoshone | 2,096,161 |
| Elmore | 1,179,906 | Washington | 1,124,406 |
| Idaho | 1,000,808 | | |
| Kootenai | 1,480,959 | Total | $25,581,305 |

## CONDENSED CLASSIFICATION OF PROPERTY ASSESSED, 1890.

| | Valuation. |
|---|---|
| Real estate and improvements | $11,173,511 |
| Railroad property | 5,358,338 |
| Live stock | 4,744,276 |
| Goods, wares, and merchandise | 1,612,615 |
| Money, bank shares, and other securities | 763,284 |
| Personal property not classified | 1,929,281 |
| Total | $25,581,305 |

Governor Shoup says:

" From the above table it will be seen that the taxable property as it appears on the assessment rolls for the fiscal year amounts to $25,581,305. The subsequent assessment rolls should add at least enough to bring the assessment up to $26,000,000. The greater part of the real estate property is assessed in the months of April and May. Since that time there has been a large advance in real estate. The property of Boise City has advanced fully 60 per cent, and there is a rapid increase in new buildings. The same may be said of all the leading towns in the State. Improved farms have also advanced very much in value since the admission of Idaho as a State.

Next year the assessment value of property will exceed this year by several millions of dollars. Lands not patented are not taxed. There are many farms under the highest state of cultivation and improvement on unsurveyed lands, on which no taxes are paid, and will not be until the land is surveyed and patents obtained. Our mines are not taxed. They represent a valuation of $50,000,000. With this large amount of unassessable property, taken together with the fact that property is not assessed at over 50 per cent of its actual valuation, it will readily be seen that not more than one-fourth of the value of the property in Idaho appears on the assessment rolls."

## PUBLIC LANDS.

The area of the State, from careful estimates, is 86,294 square miles, or 55,228,160 acres, and may be classified as follows:

|  | Acres, |
|---|---|
| Agricultural lands | 16,000,000 |
| Forest lands | 10,000,000 |
| Grazing and mineral lands | 20,000,000 |
| Rough, mountainous, unfit for cultivation | 8,000,000 |
| Lakes and rivers | 1,288,000 |
| Total | 55,228,160 |

There are within the State 13,200 square miles of valley lands situated at an elevation of less than 3,000 feet; 10,000 square miles between 3,000 and 4,000 feet; 22,000 square miles between 4,000 and 5,000 feet, and 19,200 square miles between 5,000 and 6,000 feet. It will, therefore, be observed that of a total of some 15,000,000 acres of arable lands in Idaho, 8,448,000 are valley lands. The balance are uplands, or " plains." Of the total arable area, the Boise Land District, occupying the western portion of the State, and traversed by the Oregon Short Line, contains 3,500,000 acres. Of this, 2,500,000 acres are still open to settlement. At Boise City is the Land Office for this district.

Hailey Land District in the central portion of the State, also traversed by the Oregon Short Line Division of the Union Pacific, contains about 1,000,000 acres of arable land, of which about 750,000 acres are still vacant and open to settlement. At Hailey is the Land Office for this district.

Blackfoot Land District, occupying the eastern portion of the State, and traversed by the Oregon Short Line and Utah & Northern Divisions of the Union Pacific Railway, contains about 4,500,000 acres of land susceptible of cultivation, of which 3,500,000 are still open to settlement.   At Blackfoot is the Land Office for this district.

Cœur d'Alene and Lewiston Land Districts, occupying the northern part of the Territory, and traversed by the Oregon Short Line, contain at least 2,500,000 acres of arable land, of which 1,500,000 acres are open to settlement.

The Blackfoot, Nez Perces, Lemhi, and Cœur d'Alene Indian Reservations occupy about 1,500,000 acres of the finest agricultural lands in Idaho. It is believed that but a few years will elapse before large portions of these lands will be thrown open to settlement, as the Indians are gradually becoming converted to the plan of accepting lands in severalty.   If each head of a family were given 320 acres of land, there would be enough of these reservation lands left to make 7,000 farms of 160 acres each.

Here is a princely area of some 10,000,000 acres of Government lands— more than 60,000 farms of 160 acres each, which Uncle Sam has to give away to his home-born or adopted sons in Idaho.

To give the reader a better idea of the location and nature of these lands we will add a brief description of the leading characteristics of them.   First as to the valleys.   The valleys of Idaho are all narrow, seldom being more than ten miles wide, while their length frequently extends fifty miles.   The valleys, however, are of very rich soil, and the flat bottom-lands, or the gently-rising plateaus that lie along the creek or river banks, are very productive.   Following is a list of the most prominent of these valleys, with their arable dimensions estimated by the most competent authorities:—

| NAME AND LOCATION OF VALLEY. | Length, Miles. | Breadth, Miles. |
|---|---|---|
| South Fork, Snake River, Eastern Idaho | 30 | 2 to 4 |
| Salt River Valley, Eastern Idaho | 20 | 1 to 2 |
| Bear River Valley, Eastern Idaho | 40 | 3 to 5 |
| Snake Valley, North Fork, Eastern Idaho | 60 | 2 to 10 |
| Blackfoot Valley, Eastern Idaho | 20 | 2 to 5 |
| Round Valley, Eastern Idaho | 30 | 8 to 12 |
| Wood River Valley, Central Idaho | 50 | 1 to 10 |
| Camas Prairie, Central Idaho | 70 | 18 to 25 |
| Boise Valley, Western Idaho | 60 | 2 to 6 |
| Payette Valley, Western Idaho (Including Long Valley) | 75 | 2 to 15 |
| Weiser Valley, Western Idaho | 40 | 2 to 5 |
| Lemhi Valley, Northeastern Idaho | 70 | 3 to 6 |
| Pahsimari Valley, Northeastern Idaho | 40 | 1 to 10 |
| Northern Camas Prairie, North Idaho | 30 | 20 to 25 |
| Potlach Valley, North Idaho | 25 | 10 to 15 |
| Palouse Valley, North Idaho | 20 | 5 to 10 |
| St. Joseph Valley, North Idaho | 15 | 5 to 10 |

The valleys mentioned above are not all that are suitable for settlement. We could name over a score or more in addition, where the opportunities are fully as advantageous as in these.   Beautiful little vales and cosy parks hidden among the hills, are innumerable, while sheep ranches, cattle ranches, dairy farms, poultry ranches, and apiaries could be established in a thousand localities, and will be as soon as the advantages that await the settlers in Idaho are more fully known.

The northern portion of the State, included between the Clearwater and the British Possessions, is chiefly mountainous, interspersed with prairie lands, and, as already noted, a number of lakes, some of them of exquisite beauty. Along the shores of these lakes and in the river bottoms are good arable lands. North Palouse, Genesee, Paradise, and Potlatch Valleys, in Nez Perces county, are rapidly filling up with an intelligent and thrifty farming population. In the neighborhood of Lewiston, fruits and vegetables of all kinds are raised in perfection. Peach trees have been known to bloom there in February. Lewiston and Moscow are the chief distributing points for this agricultural area.

In this North Idaho region, crops are raised without irrigation. The precipitation of moisture on the mountains is said to be greater than on the lowlands, but the hills and uplands adjacent to the great mass of mountains receive some of the supply condensed by the mountains themselves, and the lands have been found to be favored by this condition to an extent sufficient to warrant agricultural operations independent of irrigation.

The more central region, between the Boise River and the Clearwater, consists of table-lands naturally rich in grasses, heavily timbered mountains and fertile valleys. The best known of these are the Clearwater, Salmon, Payette, Weiser, Boise, Garden and Long valleys, all presenting rare opportunities for ranching and stock-raising; grain and cereals of all kinds are produced. Long Valley is seventy-five miles long and about fifteen wide. It is traversed longitudinally by the North Fork of the Payette. There are few settlements. The soil is rich, and offers excellent inducements to those desiring to go into the business of dairying and stock-raising. Upper and Lower Squaw creeks and Horseshoe Bend form one continuous valley country, where grain can be raised in abundance, and where there are ranges capable of sustaining many herds of stock. These valleys are all well watered, possessing extraordinary fertility of soil. With the aid of irrigation these lands produce abundant crops of cereals, as well as the fruits and vegetables of the Middle States. There is sufficient timber to contribute to the salubrity and humidity of the climate.

Between Boise Valley and the southern boundary line there are fertile valleys traversing sage-brush plains and table-lands. The proportion of timber in this region is small, being confined chiefly to the lines of streams and mountain sides. Three-fourths of this vast surface is capable of reclamation by irrigation, and will produce abundant crops. In the southwest section of this district are several fertile valleys tributary to the Owyhee.

The area formed by the junction of the Boise, Payette, Weiser, Snake, and Owyhee valleys, in Southwestern Idaho, is a vast agricultural region. In this immense basin, formed by the confluence of Idaho's great rivers, is a compact body of farming lands, millions of acres in extent—the largest agricultural area between the great prairies and the plains of the Columbia. In soil, climate, and facilities for irrigation it is unsurpassed. It is mainly the rich, warm loam that produces sage-brush to perfection in its natural state, and all the cereals, fruits and vegetables of this latitude when cultivated. There are acres upon acres of apples, plums, pears, peaches, and small fruits, and alongside of them, almost as far as the eye can reach, are stretches of wild farming lands awaiting claimants and cultivation. Several large canals are being constructed to water this region, notably that projected and managed by Mr Howard Sebree, near Caldwell. It is already twenty-four miles long, twenty feet wide on the bottom, and four feet deep, and affords water for a large region hitherto worthless.

South of Snake River, in Southern Central Idaho, is Goose Creek Valley, which extends north and south from Snake River to the Utah line. This is the most extentive valley in Cassia county, and one of the finest in the Territory. There are now over 3,000 acres under cultivation, and with the water that is in Goose Creek it is thought that 10,000 acres can be cultivated The valley is about five miles in width at its southern extremity, and widens quite rapidly towards the north, until it opens into Snake River Valley. Extending from Snake River up Goose Creek is a body of over 200,000 acres of the finest land, that only requires water to make it one of the best agricultural districts in the State.

Referring to this Cassia county region, a well-informed settler writes as follows: "It is bounded by latitude 42° on the south, and by Snake River on the north. Covering about 5,000 square miles of territory, more than one-half of its area is valley land. Its southern portion is crossed by mountain ranges, among which are the Sublette, Black Pine, Goose Creek, Rock, and Salmon Creek mountains, Mount Harrison and Mount Independence in the Goose Creek Range, rising to an elevation of about 10,000 feet. The most important valleys are those of Raft River, Goose Creek and Salmon Creek, although many smaller basins of surpassing beauty and fertility are found. The county is drained by Snake River and its tributaries Salmon Creek, Rock Creek, Dry Creek, Cottonwood, Goose Creek, Marsh Creek, Raft River, and many smaller streams. Lying in the central part of the Upper Mountain District, in an immense depression, traversed in every portion by the balmy Chinook winds, these valley lands possess a mild climate, healthful and pleasant as any on the footstool. Cyclones, blizzards and extreme changes of temperature are unknown. The soil, deep and fertile as the Valley of the Nile, will, with irrigation, produce all fruits, grains, and vegetables known to the temperate zone in great profusion and of surpassing excellence. Washed on the northern edge by a great river, a moderate expenditure of capital in the construction of canals and diversion of water would turn these valleys into a veritable Eden. From such canals water could be furnished to work the vast placer deposits along Snake River, and almost unlimited water-power be developed for manufacturing purposes. Recognizing all this, and realizing the benefits of such work to its full extent, the citizens of Cassia county have had a preliminary survey made for a proposed grand canal from Snake River. Said survey has demonstrated the fact that at an expenditure of much less than $5 per acre, more than 1,000,000 acres of this land can be reclaimed, and to this attractive, immensely remunerative, and entirely safe investment, the attention of capital is invited. In this county are also found large quarries of marble and building stone, promising gold, silver, lead and coal prospects. Thorough investigation and better transportation facilities will probably develop immense mines of the precious and base metals. With a sparse population at present of 4,000, this county can be made to sustain at least 200,000 inhabitants; diversified by scenery sublime, picturesque and beautiful, 'a land fair and inviting in the eyes of all men,' it must in a decade hence become the home of teeming thousands, the seat of great marts of industry and commerce, this superb and incomparable county of Cassia."

On the 19th day of July, 1888, Senator George Hearst said in the Senate of the United States: "Snake River Valley alone was estimated to be able to support 2,000,000 of people. * * * I have been over all the Territories west of the Rocky Mountains as much, perhaps, as any other man, and I think *Idaho has more agricultural land in it than. all the other Territories there.*"

Surrounding Mountain Home in Southern Central Idaho, is a tract of about 100,000 acres—nearly all Government land—of the very cream of Idaho uplands. It is unsurpassed for fertility and requires less irrigation than the average of such lands. A company is now constructing a canal to water a portion of this splendid tract. Good mining markets are convenient, and the Oregon Short Line crosses this land.

In the Wood River region are Wood River Valley and Camas Prairie, the former an ideal mountain valley, two to ten miles wide and fifty miles long, and the latter seventy miles long and twenty miles wide. This Camas Prairie is not to be confounded with the prairie of the same name in Idaho county. It is about twenty miles west of Hailey. Through its southern portion runs Camas Creek, a tributary of Wood River. The whole prairie is magnificently watered, and, in season, covered with a luxuriant growth of grass, making it a paradise for stock. The soil is a rich black loam. Irrigation is said to be unnecessary on a large portion of the lands, for the reason that there is a heavy clay sub-soil which holds the water and moisture. The resources of Camas Prairie have been thus described: "The numerous creeks which are flowing through the valley keep the clay soil wet, so that however dry the top soil may look, you will always find plenty of moisture within a few inches of the surface. In demonstration of this fact we have only to say that water in endless quantities can be found almost anywhere on the prairie, at a depth of from two to eight feet below the surface. Many settlers have wells with sufficient water for all stock at that depth. This condition of soil renders the land of this prairie very productive. Immense crops of oats, wheat, barley, and all small grain, and all kinds of vegetables and fruits can be grown easily and to great profit. The natural grasses yield wonderful crops of hay, and tame grasses, wherever tried, flourish amazingly. Timothy, alfalfa, and clover have been sown, and have proved to be big croppers and very hardy in growth. We know of fields of timothy which were sown on sod that yielded two or three tons per acre. Tame grasses and all small grains find their natural elements here, and consequently yield enormously. At Armstrong's Willow Creek ranch, in 1886, five acres of volunteer wheat yielded 522 bushels, or at the rate of over *one hundred and four bushels per acre.* This is, of course, an extreme case—in fact, it stands unequaled, even on Camas Prairie, that garden spot of Idaho—but several instances could be cited where the yield of volunteer wheat has reached seventy-five bushels per acre. The soil is so well adapted to the raising of potatoes and vegetables that a yield of less than one ton of potatoes per acre is a great dissappointment, while of rutabagas, carrots, etc., less than two tons is not considered an average crop. And this, it must be borne in mind, is in fresh plowed ground, that five years ago had never felt the tramp of civilized men. Squire Abbott, one of the residents of Camas Prairie, sowed one pound of wheat which he received from the East, and, on harvesting and cleaning up, realized *one hundred pounds* of nice, clean wheat. Barley sown on sod last year produced from fifty to sixty-five bushels to the acre, *without any irrigation*. All kinds of garden vegetables, such as beets, turnips, peas, beans, onions, cabbages, etc., are successfully and very profitably cultivated, the crop is monstrous the quality par excellence, and the market for all that is not needed for home consumption is sure, and at paying prices. In fact the soil of Camas Prairie cannot be excelled in any State or Territory in the Union." Wood River Valley requires irrigation, and many miles of canal are annually being constructed to reclaim its broad areas of rich lands.

In northwestern Idaho, agriculture ably supplements the mining industry in enriching the country. The Salmon River, rising in Sawtooth Mountains, north of Wood River, enters on its southwestern border, and pursuing a zigzag course in a general northeasterly direction, receives the waters of ten large creeks besides the East Fork. These streams, together with Lost River and its tributaries, flow through thousands of acres of arable land still uncultivated. In Round Valley, containing thirty square miles of arable and grazing land, but a small portion has been cultivated; in Lost River Valley, containing in Custer county, about 100 square miles of arable land, 4,000 acres of hay and grain were cultivated in 1887; in Pahsimari, containing about fifty square miles of arable land, comparatively none is under cultivation. A few families have settled in Pahsimari—a valley forty miles in length by ten miles in average width—but beyond a few tons of hay, grain, etc., for home use, nothing has been produced. This valley alone will furnish homes and occupation for hundreds of people. Lost River, from its source to the point where it sinks into the lava beds, runs for sixty-five miles through a fine valley, rich in natural resources. Since the mining excitement of recent years, 800 people have flocked thither—of whom, perhaps, one-half are engaged in agriculture. With homes to build, land to inclose and bring under the beneficent effects of irrigation, the newcomers still found time the first season to cut about 5,000 tons of wild hay, and raised 10,000 bushels of grain. The grain crop this year will quadruple this amount. Farming in Round Valley has been liberally rewarded. The acreage under cultivation has steadily increased for five years, until this year its contribution to the county's wealth is 30,000 bushels of grain, and 800 tons of hay, besides thousands of pounds of vegetables. Men who came here penniless a few years ago, now own ranches with houses, equipments, and live stock and are worth from $3,000 to $15,000.

## PRICES PAID FOR CROPS.

Oats is the principal grain raised in northeastern Idaho, being of a very hardy, solid character, and for that reason taking the place of barley. Wheat could be raised as profitably as oats, if there were only flour mills in the country to grind it. There is no lack of a market, as 400,000 pounds of flour are annually imported to meet the consumption, at prices ranging from $4.50 to $6 per hundred, according to locality and season. Hay yields about one and a half tons to the acre, in its wild state. Alfalfa, blue-grass, red-top, and timothy have been successfully sown. The profits accruing to farmers will give no surprise, when it is understood that oats bring $1.25 per bushel; hay, $20 per ton; potatoes, 2 cents per pound; cabbage, 4 cents; onions, 8 cents, and turnips, 1 cent per pound. Other farm produce is sold as follows: Eggs at 50 cents per dozen; butter at 40 to 50 cents per pound, and chickens at 50 cents apiece. Not only is a ready market found at these prices, but annually thousands of dollars' worth of hay, grain, butter, eggs, and poultry are imported from other countries, or Utah, to meet home demand. Hereafter, the tendency of prices will be slightly downward, still the margin left for profits will be extraordinarily large.

Lemhi Valley, the largest, best settled, and most extensively cultivated valley in northeastern Idaho, is seventy miles in length, and varies in width from three to six miles, comprising within its limits, bottom and bench lands of unsurpassed fertility, adapted by reason of its low altitude and sheltered situation to the successful cultivation of all cereals, vegetables, and fruits. The principal crops raised in Lemhi Valley are wheat, oats, barley, and potatoes. The wheat crop of Lemhi Valley has never yet proved a failure, yielding from forty to fifty bushels of fine, hard, No. 1 wheat, weighing fifty-eight to sixty-two and one-half pounds to the bushel. A steadily increasing home-demand has created a good market at $1.20 per bushel. This has been the ruling price for a number of years. Oats have been for years a never-failing crop, yielding from forty-five to fifty-five bushels to the acre, of heavy, full kernels, weighing forty-five pounds to the bushel, and commanding ready sale at from 1½ to 2 cents per pound, with the demand always in excess of the supply. Barley has been but little cultivated, although as safe and certain a crop as wheat or oats, yielding from thirty-five to forty-five bushels to the acre, and selling at 2 cents per pound. Lemhi valley has been justly famous for the superior quality of potatoes grown there, finding a ready market and sale everywhere in the mining camps. The yield of potatoes in this valley has averaged over 250 bushels to the acre, and the market price varies from $1.50 to $4.50 per hundred pounds, according to season. The writer has seen some of these tubers weighing four pounds and eight ounces, and was assured by the producer that he had bushels of the same kind in the field, all sound and solid potatoes. During the seventeen years in which Lemhi Valley has been farmed, no failure of this crop has ever been reported.

Then in Eastern Idaho are Bear Valley, Snake Valley, Malad Valley, and others, altogether affording room for thousands of settlers, who will find the condition much the same as in the other valleys described. The

Snake Valley, near Eagle Rock, and Blackfoot, the largest irrigating canals
in the State, are being constructed, reclaiming lands for many new settlers.   This is the famous potato region from which about 1,000 car-loads of
potatoes are marketed annually.

It should also be remembered that the mountain slopes of Idaho are
watered by abundant streams, and checkered with alternate tracts of forest and rich prairie.   Even in the least favored regions are localities
adapted to specific branches of agricultural enterprise.   These will ulti-
mately be occupied by a thrifty farming population who are not afraid of
severe winters—for it is here that the snow-fall is greatest, and the growing season short.

## HOW TO OBTAIN GOVERNMENT LAND.

PRE-EMPTION.—Heads of families, widows, or single persons (male or
female) over the age of twenty-one years, citizens of the United States or
who have declared their intention to become such, may enter and purchase
not exceeding 160 acres under the pre-emption laws.   A fee of $3 is required
within thirty days after making settlement, and within one year, actual
residences and cultivation of the tract must be shown, whereupon the pre-
emptor is entitled to purchase the same at $1.25 per acre.   A pre-emptor
may submit proofs of residence at any time after six months and obtain title
to his land.

HOMESTEADS.—Any person qualified as above is entitled to enter a
quarter section (160 acres), or less quantity of public land, under the homestead laws.   The applicant must pay the legal fee and that part of the com-
missions required, as follows:   Fee for 160 acres, $10; commission, $6; fee
for 80 acres, $5; commission, $4.   Within six months the homesteader must
take up his residence upon the land and reside thereupon, and cultivate the
same for five years continuously.   Final proof cannot be made until the
expiration of five years from date of entry, and must be made within seven
years.   A settler may prove his residence at any time after six months and
purchase the land under the pre-emption laws, if desired.

TREE CLAIMS.—Under the timber culture laws, not more than 160
acres on any one section, entirely devoid of timber can be entered.   The
qualifications of applicants are the same as under the pre-emption and
homestead laws.   Land-office charges are $14 for 160 acres or more than
80 acres, when entry is made, and $4 at final proof.   Land to be entered
must be entirely devoid of timber.   Party making entry of 160 acres is
required to break or plow five acres during the first year and five acres
during the second year.   The five acres broken or plowed the first year
must be cultivated the second year, and be planted in timber during the
third year.   The five acres broken or plowed the second year, must be
cultivated the third year and planted in timber the fourth year.   At the
end of eight years, or within two years after that period, proof by two
creditable witnesses must be adduced, showing that there were at the end
of eight years, at least 675 living, thrifty trees on each of the ten acres

required to be planted; also not less than 2,700 trees were planted to each of the ten acres. Fruit trees are not considered timber within the meaning of this act.

DESERT LAND ACT.—Any person possessing the aforesaid qualifications may file his oath with the Register and Receiver of the land office in the district in which any land is located that he intends to reclaim, not to exceed 640 acres of said land, in a compact form, by conducting water upon it within three years of the date of the said oath, and by paying to the Receiver the sum of 25 cents per acre for all the land claimed, may enter said lands under the Desert Land Act. At any time within three years a patent can be obtained by making proof that he has reclaimed said land, and paying the additional sum of $1 per acre. This act applies to desert lands in Dakota, Montana, Idaho, Washington and Oregon.

All these acts are liable to be materially changed—some of them repealed —during 1891. Much more stringent conditions will be placed upon the disposal of all public lands. It therefore behooves the homeseeker to make his choice of government land quickly.

## RAILWAYS.

Idaho is now thoroughly accessible from either the east or west, via the Union Pacific System. The great through Portland route of the Union Pacific conveys the passengers from the Missouri River to the most remote station in Idaho in three days, while from Portland eastward to the heart of the State consumes only twenty-four hours. Salt Lake City is reached in twenty-four hours, and San Francisco in about sixty-five hours.

OREGON SHORT LINE RAILWAY COMPANY.—The Oregon Short Line is the most important railroad in the State, carrying, as it does, all the through traffic passing over the Union Pacific Railway System from the North Pacific coast for all points on the Atlantic seaboard, and to all intermediate points. The volume of tonnage and local business is increasing each year. This road enters the State on the Wyoming line near the town of Montpelier, passing through the counties of Bear Lake, Bingham, Logan, Elmore, Ada, and Washington, to the town of Huntington, on the border of the State of Oregon, a distance of 465.63 miles.

The first place of importance on the line of this road is Montpelier, in Bear Lake county. This town has a population of over 1,000 inhabitants. The people of the town and surrounding country are industrious. It is the center of a large agricultural district. A large number of cattle, horses and sheep, together with a heavy tonnage of grain, are shipped annually from this town.

Soda Springs is the next place of importance, and furnishes for Eastern markets horses, cattle and sheep. Hay and grain are also shipped in considerable quantity. The famous soda or mineral springs at this place are receiving merited and wide-spread notice. About 1,000,000 bottles of this superior mineral water have been marketed during the past year.

McCammon, at the junction of the Utah and Northern Railway, supplies a large amount of tonnage of both stock and grain.

Pocatello is on the Fort Hall Indian Reservation. The Indians have here ceded their right to about 1,800 acres of land for a town site, which has been surveyed and platted under the supervision of the general government. The population of Pocatello is about 1,500, and is in the heart of a fine agricultural district. The great body of the land is, however, covered by the Indian Reservation. The shipment of grain is, therefore, small. Stock of all kinds is shipped in considerable quantities.

The Utah and Northern Railway diverges from the Oregon Short Line at this station, running northward to the Montana line. From McCammon to Pocatello these roads run on the same road bed.

American Falls, on the western border of the Indian Reservation, furnishes horses, cattle and sheep in large numbers for transportation to market.

Located at the junction of the Wood River branch with the Oregon Short Line is the beautiful and prosperous town of Shoshone. Railway shipments in this town in grain, wool, hay, and stock of all kinds are steadily increasing. It is surrounded on all sides by excellent agricultural lands. The celebrated and wonderful Shoshone Falls on the Snake River are about twenty miles distant from this town. A line of coaches runs between the two places.

Glenn's Ferry and Mountain Home are prominent for both shipping and distributing points, and are growing towns of importance.

Nampa is about twenty miles from Boise City, the capital of the State, and is the junction of the Idaho Central Railway with the main line. Nampa has doubled its population, business and buildings during the past year. It is in the center of one of the finest agricultural districts on the line of the road and distributes to a large area of country. A stage line runs from this place to Silver City, De Lamar, and other points south.

Caldwell is one of the most prosperous towns on the line of this road. Many new buildings have been constructed during the year, and business in all branches is reported to have increased 50 per cent over last year. Outgoing and incoming shipments show a large increase over the past year. A large and very prosperous agricultural area is tributary to this place. Large quantities of grain, hay, wool, and stock of all kinds are shipped.

Payette is a prosperous town and surrounded, like Caldwell, by a rich agricultural country. The volume of its business has increased very much during the year. Some of the most prosperous settlements in the State are tributary to this town. Shipments of all kinds of farm products, wool, and stock show a most gratifying gain.

Weiser, the last town of importance on this road, was, during the early part of the summer, nearly destroyed by fire. It is rapidly rebuilding, and a better class of buildings is taking the place of those destroyed. It is similarly surrounded as the towns last named. The merchants of this place are energetic and report a large increase of business over last year. In addition to the fine agricultural lands tributary to Weiser, extensive and rich mines have been discovered and are being vigorously worked. It will, before long, be one of the most prosperous towns on the line of this road.

OREGON SHORT LINE RAILWAY.

| COUNTIES. | Miles. | Valuation per mile. | Aggregate valuation. |
|---|---|---|---|
| Bear Lake............................................................ | 45.48 | $6,500 | $ 295,620 |
| Oneida ................................................................ | 21.44 | 6,500 | 139,360 |
| Bingham ............................................................. | 58.31 | 6,500 | 379,015 |
| Logan.......... ..................................................... | 117.67 | 6,500 | 764,855 |
| Elmore .............................................................. | 64.67 | 6,500 | 420,355 |
| Ada..................................................................... | 75.58 | 6,500 | 491,270 |
| Washington........................................................ | 28.10 | 6,500 | 182,650 |
| Total................................................... | 411.25 | .................... | $2,673,125 |

UTAH AND NORTHERN.—This railway enters Idaho from near the town of Franklin, in this State, passing northerly through the counties of Oneida and Bingham to the Montana line. In 1889 76.87 miles were narrow gauge and 129.62 standard gauge. Since that date the narrow gauge has been changed to standard gauge. In several places on the line of the road a new road-bed has been graded, which has shortened the line by several miles.

There is no material change to report on the through business of this road. There is a marked improvement, however, to note in local traffic. The town of Franklin, near the Utah line, has increased her shipments of cereals and stock very materially. The shipments to and from Pocatello have also increased.

The town of Blackfoot, in the great Snake River Valley, has made marked progress during the year. The export of grain, hay, wool, and stock of all kinds will exceed that of former seasons. A much larger area than ever before of the fine agricultural land surrounding it has been reclaimed during the year. The harvests have been abundant and the people prosperous. It is the distributing point for a large district and is the principal shipping point for Custer county.

Eagle Rock is located at the point where this road crosses Snake River, and has the advantage of being the shipping point of the largest agricultural district in the eastern part of the State. It is believed that more agricultural land has been reclaimed tributary to this station during the past year than in any other district in the State. Shipments of flour, grain, wool and stock exceed former years.

Camas is surrounded by an excellent grazing country and is the supply depot for several mining camps.

Beaver Cañon, at the foot of the Continental Divide, is noted for the large amount of lumber sawed and shipped to stations along the line of the road. Many of the National Park tourists leave the railroad at this point.

UTAH & NORTHERN RAILWAY COMPANY.

| COUNTIES. | Miles. | Valuation per mile. | Aggregate valuation. |
|---|---|---|---|
| Narrow Gauge: | | | |
| Bingham | 55.42 | $5,000 | $277,100 |
| Oneida | 21.45 | 5,000 | 107,250 |
| | 76.87 | | $384,350 |
| Standard Gauge, Bingham | 129.62 | $6,500 | 842,530 |
| Total valuation | | | $1,226,880 |

WOOD RIVER BRANCH OF THE OREGON SHORT LINE RAILWAY.—This road is a branch of the Oregon Short Line, leaving the main line at the town of Shoshone, in Logan county, and terminating at Ketchum, in Alturas county. Total length of road is 69.96 miles.

Bellevue, on the line of this road, is an important supply and shipping point for a large number of valuable mining properties. The shipment of ores and concentrates for the present year is larger than for 1889. Stimulated by the advance of silver and lead, the owners of many low-grade mines will make larger shipments during the next year than ever before. Bellevue is at the base of a low range of mountains, and has a good ranch and grain trade. The town is prosperous, showing a marked improvement over last year.

Hailey is the county seat of Alturas county. One year ago it was in ashes, but substantial brick blocks have sprung up over the ruins. It is a distributing point for a large mining district. Surrounded on all sides by vast mineral belts, this town will continue to grow, business will increase, and the road will be satisfied with the traffic to and from this point.

Ketchum, the terminal point of the road, is the supply station for an extensive region. Supplies are distributed for an extensive mining district, and it is one of the principal shipping points for Challis, Clayton, Custer, Bonanza, and other important places in Custer county. There are large reduction works and smelters near the town.

WOOD RIVER RAILWAY.

| COUNTIES. | Miles. | Valuation per mile. | Aggregate valuation. |
|---|---|---|---|
| Logan | 54.38 | $6,500 | $353,470 |
| Alturas | 15.58 | 6,500 | 101,270 |
| Total | 69.96 | | $454,740 |

IDAHO CENTRAL RAILWAY.—This is a branch of the Oregon Short Line system, leaving the main line at Nampa and terminating at Boisé City, the capital of the State. The tonnage and travel over this road have more than doubled during the past year. This result is brought about by the large number of new buildings erected at the capital during the year, also the large increase of business reported by merchants.

IDAHO CENTRAL RAILWAY.

| COUNTY. | Miles. | Valuation per mile. | Aggregate valuation. |
|---|---|---|---|
| Ada | 18.94 | $3,000 | $56,820 |

SPOKANE FALLS AND IDAHO RAILWAY COMPANY.—This railway connects with the Northern Pacific Railway near the Idaho line, running thence to Cœur d'Alene City, on the border of Lake Cœur d'Alene, where it connects with the line of steamboats plying between Cœur d'Alene City and old Mission on Cœur d'Alene River. Until the present season this road, with the steamboat line and the Cœur d'Alene Railway & Navigation Company, had the exclusive carrying trade of the Cœur d'Alene mines. Since the completion of the Washington & Idaho road into the Cœur d'Alene mines the business seems to be nearly equally divided.

SPOKANE FALLS AND IDAHO RAILWAY COMPANY.

| COUNTY. | Miles. | Valuation per mile. | Aggregate valuation. |
|---|---|---|---|
| Kootenai | 13.50 | $3,000 | $40,500 |

CŒUR D'ALENE RAILWAY & NAVIGATION COMPANY.—This road commences at the old Cœur d'Alene Mission near the head of navigation on the Cœur d'Alene River, running through the towns of Kingston, Wardner Junction, Osborne, and Wallace to Murray, with a short branch to Burke. It parallels the Washington & Idaho Railway, and is a competitor for patronage in the same field and towns in the great Cœur d'Alene country. It is narrow gauge, and connects with a line of steam-boats plying between Cœur d'Alene Mission and Cœur d'Alene City.

CŒUR D'ALENE RAILWAY AND NAVIGATION COMPANY.

| COUNTIES. | Miles. | Valuation per mile. | Aggregate valuation. |
|---|---|---|---|
| Kootenai | 2.10 | $5,000 | $ 10,500 |
| Shoshone | 36.43 | 5,000 | 182,150 |
| Totals | 38.53 | .............. | $192,650 |

Spokane & Palouse Railway.—This road enters the State in Nez Perces county in township 37, range 6, terminating at the town of Genesee, in Latah county. It penetrates the finest wheat belt in the State, if not in the world, and is a supply road for the Northern Pacific system.

SPOKANE AND PALOUSE RAILWAY.

| COUNTIES. | Miles. | Valuation per mile. | Aggregate valuation. |
|---|---|---|---|
| Nez Perces | 5.66 | $6,500 | $36,790 |
| Latah | 1.47 | 6,500 | 9,555 |
| Total | 7.13 | | $46,345 |

Oregon Railway & Navigation Company.—This road is a supply branch or feeder of the Union Pacific system, entering the State about 2½ miles west of Moscow, the thrifty county seat of Latah county. There are but 2½ miles of this road in the State. Its business, however, is marvelous. Moscow is in the heart of the great wheat belt of this favored region. Wheat, oats, barley, flaxseed, stock, brick and lumber are the principal articles of commerce. Moscow will have another railroad before the close of the present season.

OREGON RAILWAY AND NAVIGATION COMPANY.

| COUNTY. | Miles. | Valuation per mile. | Aggregate valuation. |
|---|---|---|---|
| Latah | 2.50 | $9,080 | $22,700 |

Washington & Idaho Railway Company.—This line starts from Farmington, State of Washington, and runs easterly through the Cœur d'Alene Indian Reservation, up the valley of the main Cœur d'Alene river, and thence up to the South Fork of the same river to the town of Mullan, in Shoshone county, passing through the prosperous towns of Wardner Junction, Osborne and Wallace. Each of the towns named are large shippers of "silver-lead ores." The mining camps surrounding these towns are the most productive in the State. Considerable grading has been done on this road between Mullan and the Montana line.

WASHINGTON AND IDAHO RAILWAY COMPANY.

| COUNTIES. | Miles. | Valuation per mile. | Aggregate valuation. |
|---|---|---|---|
| Kootenai | 55.32 | $6,500 | $359,580 |
| Shoshone | 29.65 | 6,500 | 192,725 |
| Total | 84.97 | | $552,305 |

## TOTAL MILEAGE OF RAILWAYS IN THE STATE.

| COUNTIES. | NAME OF RAILWAY. | Miles in county. | Value per mile. | Aggregate assessed valuation. |
|---|---|---|---|---|
| Bear Lake........ ...... | Oregon Short Line............................. | *45.48 | $6,500 | $295,620 |
| Bingham ............ | " " ............................... | *58.31 | 6,500 | 379,015 |
| Logan ............... | " " ............................... | *172.05 | 6,500 | 1,118,325 |
| Alturas ................... | " " ............................... | *15.58 | 6,500 | 101,270 |
| Elmore ........... | " " ............................... | *64.67 | 6,500 | 420,355 |
| Oneida.................. | " " ............................... | *21.44 | 6,500 | 139,360 |
| Ada.............. | " " ............................... | *75.58 | 6,500 | 491,270 |
| Washington.... .... | " " ............................... | *28.10 | 6,500 | 182,650 |
| Oneida.............. | Utah and Northern ....................... | †21.45 | 5,000 | 107,250 |
| Bingham ............ | " " ............................... | †55.42 | 5,000 | 277,100 |
| " | " " ............................... | *129.62 | 6,500 | 842,530 |
| Ada ................. | Idaho Central............................. | 18.94 | 3,000 | 56,820 |
| Nez Pérces........... | Spokane and Palouse.................... | *5.66 | 6,500 | 36,790 |
| Latah ................... | " " ............................... | *1.47 | 6,500 | 9,555 |
| " ................ | Oregon Railway and Navigation Co.. | 2.50 | ............. | 22,700 |
| Kootenai ............ | Washington and Idaho.................... | *55.32 | 6,500 | 359,580 |
| Shoshone ............ | " " ............................... | *29.65 | 6,500 | 192,725 |
| Kootenai ............ | Cœur d'Alene Railway and Nav. Co.. | 12.10 | 5,000 | 10,500 |
| Shoshone ............ | " " ............................... | †36.43 | 5,000 | 182,150 |
| Kootenai ............ | Northern Pacific......................... | 88.00 | ............. | ...................... |
| " ............... | Spokane Falls and Idaho................ | 13.50 | 3,000 | 40,500 |
| Total........... | .................................................... | 941.27 | ............. | $5,266,065 |

*Standard Gauge.                    †Narrow Gauge.

## TELEGRAPH LINES IN THE STATE.

| COUNTIES. | NAME OF TELEGRAPH COMPANY. | Wires. | Miles in county. | Value per mile. | Aggregate valuation. |
|---|---|---|---|---|---|
| Ada...................... | Silver City Telegraph Co.......... | 1 | 20.00 | $ 30 | $ 600 00 |
| Owyhee................. | " | 1 | 27.00 | 30 | 810 00 |
| Alturas ................. | Western Union Telegraph Co... | 1 | 15.38 | 50 | 769 00 |
| Bear Lake............ | " .............................. | 1 | 22.04 | 50 | 1,102 00 |
| Kootenai............. | " ............:................ | 1 | 78.00 | 50 | 3,900 00 |
| Logan................... | " .............................. | 1 | 54.38 | 50 | 2,719 00 |
| Latah ................ | " .............................. | 1 | 3.00 | 50 | 150 00 |
| Ada .................... | " .............................. | 2 | 95.47 | 70 | 6,682 90 |
| Bear Lake............ | " .............................. | 2 | 23.30 | 70 | 1,631 00 |
| Bingham.............. | " .............................. | 2 | 57.72 | 70 | 4,040 40 |
| Elmore................. | " .............................. | 2 | 64.67 | 70 | 4,526 90 |
| Logan................... | " .............................. | 2 | 117.67 | 70 | 8,236 90 |
| Oneida................. | " .............................. | 2 | 21.97 | 70 | 1,537 90 |
| Washington........ | " .............................. | 2 | 28.08 | 70 | 1,965 60 |
| Bingham.............. | " .............................. | 4 | 162.24 | 110 | 17,846 40 |
| Oneida................. | " .............................. | 4 | 21.45 | 110 | 2,359 50 |
| Kootenai............. | " .............................. | 5 | 58.00 | 130 | 7,540 00 |
| Bingham.............. | " .............................. | 6 | 22.80 | 150 | 3,420 00 |
| Elmore................. | Rocky Bar and Mount Home Telegraph Co....................... | ............ | 54.00 | 25 | 1,350 00 |
| Total........... | .................................................... | ............ | 947.17 | ............. | $71,187 50 |

## COMMERCE.

### PRODUCTS EXPORTED BY RAILROADS FOR THE YEAR ENDING JUNE 30, 1890.

|  | Tons. |
|---|---:|
| The Union Pacific system (central and eastern Idaho) | *47,961 |
| Oregon Railway and Navigation Company | †14,740 |
| Spokane and Palouse Railway Company | †16,170 |
| Spokane Falls and Idaho Railway Company | †8,000 |
| Cœur d'Alene Railway and Navigation Company | *51,216 |
| Northern Pacific Railway Company | †12,000 |
| Washington and Idaho Railway Company | †28,000 |
| Steamboats | †24,000 |
| Total | 202,087 |

### PRODUCTS IMPORTED FOR YEAR ENDING JUNE 30, 1890.

|  | Tons. |
|---|---:|
| The Union Pacific system (central and eastern Idaho) | *67,105 |
| Oregon Railway and Navigation Company | †14,650 |
| Spokane and Palouse Railway Company | †18,500 |
| Spokane Falls and Idaho Railway Company | †7,000 |
| Cœur d'Alene Railway and Navigation Company | *28,109 |
| Northern Pacific Railway Company | †7,500 |
| Washington and Idaho Railway Company | †27,000 |
| Steamboats | †14,000 |
| Total | 183,864 |

### VALUE OF HOME PRODUCTS MARKETED FOR THE YEAR 1890.

|  |  |
|---|---:|
| Cattle, horses and sheep | $ 2,402,300 |
| Wool, pelts and hides | 885,000 |
| Grain, hay and seeds | 3,852,700 |
| Fruits and vegetables | 324,000 |
| Lumber | 1,945,600 |
| Brick and other building material | 985,550 |
| Total | $10,395,150 |

*Official.          †Estimated.

## MINING.

Hon. George L. Shoup, Governor of Idaho, in his exhaustive report for 1889, to the Secretary of the interior, said:

"Mining is the principal industry of the Territory and goes hand in hand with our growing agricultural industry. To the mines is due the first stimulus that was given to immigration. And now that mining has become as legitimate an occupation as farming, stock-raising. or any other occupation, there is less of that reckless speculation than there was a few years past. The past year has been one of hardship to many who are engaged in working placer or surface mines, caused by the unprecedented light fall of snow in the mountains last winter, thereby producing little water for this class of mining, and in some localities the supply was so light that the mines have not been touched this season. With an average water supply through the season the output of gold and silver would have been increased at least $2,000,000 more than the amount reported.

"A number of quartz-mills have been shut down for some months from the same cause. Notwithstanding the short supply of water, and the falling off of production in some localities, the yield of valuable metals in the Territory at large is most satisfactory, and is nearly double that of last year. The large increase comes from Shoshone county, where we have now developed some of the finest mines known to exist. Some of the mines have been developed for some time, but the owners were content to wait the completion of a railroad near them. The high per cent they carry in lead contributes to make the tonnage very large. From the present outlook, the production next year of gold, silver, lead, and copper will be increased over this by several million dollars. I am sincere in stating that I believe Idaho will, in a few years, lead the list of States producing gold, silver, and lead. Large copper mines have been opened in the Seven Devils district, in Washington county; also on Big and Little Lost Rivers and Birch Creek, in Alturas, Bingham and Custer counties. These mines, while high grade, are too far from railroads to be worked with profit at present. Companies are looking over the field with a view of constructing lines to them."

In his report for 1890, Governor Shoup has this to say concerning the mining interests of Idaho:

"Since the discovery of gold in Idaho by Capt. James Pearce and party on Oro Fino Creek, in 1860, the mines of Idaho have produced to date about $175,000,000. The mountains of Elmore, Boise and Ada have each hundreds of gold and silver mines. The two former counties have several mills in operation and will have several more next season. Boise county has also large placer fields.

"Owyhee county is one of the oldest quartz mining districts in Idaho, but high freights and the expense of operating mines and mills has been so great that many of the mines were abandoned, or for many years only the assessment work done on them. Recently new life has been infused into this district and systematic work resumed, developing some of the finest properties in the State. The Wilson group, owned and operated by Capt. De Lamar, has developed several very large veins, the largest of which is 75 feet between walls, and every pound is worked through the mill. There is a 20-stamp mill on this property which has produced over $800,000 in the past year, and nearly all of this large amount from development work alone. There are several million dollars worth of ore in sight. Several other mines near Silver City are paying well and have developed extensive bodies of ore.

"Gold, silver and lead mining is yet in infancy in Idaho. In my opinion, before many years, this will be the most extensive, most productive and best paying mining region in the world. There is yet in the State, in addition to the class of mines above referred to, thousands of acres of placer mines, prospected, but otherwise scarcely touched. These extensive fields are so high above or so distant from water, that they are beyond the reach of the individual miner, but in time capital will be employed to cover them with water. The sands of Snake River contain millions of dollars of fine scales of flour gold. As yet miners have been unable to save this gold by the present methods or machinery used in placer mining, or at most only a small percentage of it. This problem, without doubt, will ere long be solved.

"In the Seven Devils mining district, located in Washington county, are some of the largest and most extensive veins of copper ore known to exist. At present these mines are too far distant from railway transportation to be worked with much profit. About $50,000 worth of this ore was shipped this year. I have seen pieces of ore from one of these mines, the South Peacock; with free gold exposed to sight."

## TOTAL PRODUCTION OF GOLD, SILVER, LEAD, AND COPPER IN IDAHO FOR 1889 AND 1890.

Prepared from the reports of producers and other authentic sources.

| Counties. | Value of gold. | Value of silver. | Value of lead, at 4 cents per pound. | Value of copper, at 10 cents per pound. | Total value. |
|---|---|---|---|---|---|
| Ada | $ 5,500 | $ 500 | | | $ 6,000 |
| Alturas | 155,000 | 620,000 | $ 275,000 | | 1,050,000 |
| Bingham | 55,000 | | | | 55,000 |
| Boise | 365,000 | 253,000 | | | 618,000 |
| Cassia | 35,000 | | | | 35,000 |
| Custer | 460,000 | 2,100,000 | 160,000 | $25,600 | 2,745,600 |
| Elmore | 375,000 | 22,000 | | | 397,000 |
| Idaho | 475,000 | 35,000 | | | 510,000 |
| Kootenai | 30,000 | 60,000 | 55,000 | | 145,000 |
| Lemhi | 425,000 | 274,000 | 400,000 | | 1,099,000 |
| Logan | 57,000 | 320,000 | 80,000 | | 457,000 |
| Owyhee | 155,000 | 345,000 | | | 500,000 |
| Shoshone | 600,000 | 3,510,000 | 5,520,000 | | 9,639,000 |
| Washington | 12,000 | 25,000 | | 60,000 | 97,000 |
| Total | $3,204,500 | $7,564,500 | $6,490,000 | $85,600 | $17,344,600 |
| The returns by counties for 1890 are not available, but the total output was as follows | $ 3,595,333 | $3,594,167 | $4,510,000 | $125,000 | $13,824,500 |

## PRODUCTIONS OF THE VALUABLE METALS IN IDAHO ANNUALLY TO DATE.

| | | | |
|---|---|---|---|
| 1862 | $ 5,000,000 00 | 1878 | $ 2,657,216 91 |
| 1863 | 7,448,400 91 | 1879 | 2,553,634 58 |
| 1864 | 9,019,704 30 | 1880 | 1,634,637 19 |
| 1865 | 12,914,364 25 | 1881 | 4,915,100 00 |
| 1866 | 10,001,850 44 | 1882 | 5,500,000 00 |
| 1867 | 7,388,064 31 | 1883 | 5,000,000 00 |
| 1868 | 3,030,213 56 | 1884 | 6,500,000 00 |
| 1869 | 1,613,453 68 | 1885 | 5,755,602 00 |
| 1870 | 2,239,190 61 | 1886 | 9,679,500 00 |
| 1871 | 2,219,937 94 | 1887 | 9,245,589 00 |
| 1872 | 2,675,192 00 | 1888 | 8,905,136 00 |
| 1873 | 3,653,605 15 | 1889 | 17,344,600 00 |
| 1874 | 3,100,447 69 | 1890 | 13,824,500 00 |
| 1875 | 1,983,720 27 | | |
| 1876 | 2,267,013 36 | Total production | $171,545,462 84 |
| 1877 | 3,474,787 69 | | |

## LABOR.

Governor Shoup says:—

"There are but few new features to report on this subject, the supply keeping nearly even pace with the demand. Laborers of all classes find ready employment in the mines, logging and wood camps, teaming, farming and other industries.

"The average miner is paid $3 to $3.50 per day; the more skilful miners are paid $4 to $5 per day; mill and smelting hands are paid $3 to $4 per day; loggers, wood-choppers and saw-mill hands are paid $2 to $3.50 per day; mechanics and skilled labor, $4 to $6 per day; teamsters, $40 to $60 per month and board; laborers, $30 to $50 per month and board; farm hands, $30 to $45 per month and board; teachers, $40 to $100 per month; clerks and book-keepers, $50 to $150 per month. There continues to be a scarcity of female servants, who would get ready employment at $20 to $30 per month.

"The mining population is nearly evenly divided between Americans and men of foreign birth. The majority of foreigners are natives of Wales, Ireland, England, France, Norway, Sweden, and Germany. The majority of farm hands are of American birth, all of the States being represented, with a large percentage from the Middle and Western States. In some sections there is a considerable number of Germans, Swedes, and Norwegians, with a very few from other foreign nations, employed. Idaho has as intelligent a class of laborers as are found in any part of the United States. There has been no collision between capital and labor reported during the past year. The Chinese are rapidly leaving the Territory, being seldom employed, except as cooks and laundrymen. The majority of those remaining in the Territory, work low-grade placer mines purchased from white men.

"Our farmers are intelligent and prosperous, the majority being Americans. Their homes are surrounded with greater comforts than usually found in new countries. They are industrious, happy, and contented. What is said of the farmer, may be said of all other classes of citizens of the Territory. Intelligence, good morals, and good society are notable as the principal features of the people of Idaho.

## "IRRIGATION.

"The application of water to the arid lands of the Territory has demonstrated beyond question the 'great productiveness of the soil. Millions of acres of land in Idaho, plains and plateaus, once classified as a great desert, have been proven to be as fine agricultural land, when irrigated, as found in any part of the United States.

"The great problem has been and is now: How can water be conveyed to lands lying high above, and in many localities far distant from streams from whence the water must be brought to irrigate? Another grave question is: How can the water that goes to waste for more than one-half the year be garnered to be used during the season of irrigation? These are questions that should be considered, not for the present requirement only, but look to the welfare of the generations to follow.

"The vitality of agriculture and peace and prosperity of those engaged in cultivating the soil are deeply concerned in the solution of this great question, which has to-day a greater significance to the settlement of our lands and populating the Territories than any other.

"Prompt and decisive action should be taken looking to the control and application of water under some well formulated system. Each year's delay renders any general system more difficult for the reason that hundreds of additional water-rights have been filed. To reconcile all those claiming priority of right is a question also to be considered in the adoption of a general system.

" I do not feel justified in giving my views as to the best method of handling this important question pending the report of the Senate Committee on Irrigation. Inasmuch as the act of Congress, at its last session, in making a liberal appropriation for the survey of the arid regions, with a view to the supply of water for irrigation, was so expressed as to give prominence to reservoirs and but slight reference to surveys for canals and ditches, it was feared the Geological Bureau might so construe the act as omitting canal surveys altogether. To counteract such a construction, if found necessary, and to get the work of surveying begun in Idaho as early as possible, were subjects of especial concern, and received immediate attention through a timely report made in February last to the Department, by the surveyor-general, presenting some of the features of portions of Idaho which are similar to those of any other State or Territory. Thus was official attention directed to Idaho, and an early commencement of irrigation surveys here satisfactorily obtained.

"The action of the Senate in appointing an able and efficient committee of its members to visit, personally inspect, and report on the whole subject of the reclamation of our arid region will give us strength in the halls of Congress and educate the whole country to the fact that our arid region has arable land enough for a kingdom, and our dry, basaltic soil is the best in the world. Water is about all the fertilizer it will ever need."

## THE STATE BY COUNTIES IN 1890.

### ADA COUNTY.

|  | Assessment Values. |
|---|---|
| Improved land patented, 95,600 acres | $ 841,267 |
| Improvements on above | 811,255 |
| Improvements on unpatented land, 41,200 acres | 388,580 |
| Oregon Short Line Railway Company | 491,270 |
| Idaho Central Railway Company | 56,820 |
| Western Union Telegraph Company | 6,682 |
| Silver City Telephone Company | 600 |
| Rocky Mountain Bell Telephone Company | 3,500 |
| Irrigating canals | 30,125 |
| Money on hand | 42,365 |
| Bank-stock shares | 122,500 |
| 12,140 stock cattle at $12 | 145,680 |
| 1,375 American cows at $20 | 27,500 |
| Farming utensils | 7,300 |
| Fixtures | 6,450 |
| Furniture | 23,135 |
| Goods, wares and merchandise | 233,421 |
| Harness, robes and saddles | 3,800 |
| 1,235 hogs at $3 | 3,705 |
| 7,365 American horses at $25 | 184,125 |
| Lumber | 8,500 |
| Machinery | 17,675 |
| 175 mules at $40 | 7,000 |
| Musical instruments | 7,300 |
| 34,400 graded sheep at $2 | 68,800 |
| Solvent credits | 82,370 |
| Wagons and vehicles | 24,674 |
| Watches | 5,100 |
| Wood | 6,500 |
| Total valuation | $3,656,999 |

The county of Ada occupies a central portion of the western part of the State. It is 75 miles in length from north to south, with an average width of 35 miles. The older settlements occupy the valleys, and these valleys are thronged with prosperous people. The homes are surrounded with orchards and groves, and are sustained by fruitage from fields producing far in excess of the prairie lands of Illinois. Settlement has but fairly begun upon the uplands, and their adaptability to horticulture is yet under experiment; but the yield of grass and grain is equal to that of the valleys. More than 600,000 acres of excellent land are open to set-. tlement in this county, all of which is still owned by the Government, and subject to entry under the public land laws. Not an acre can be bought without first bringing the land under cultivation. Perhaps 10 per cent of the land of Ada county is hilly or mountainous. All of the remainder will yet be irrigated by great canals and nourish by their products tens of thousands of people.

The system of irrigating canals already provided is the wonder of all who visit this prosperous county. Small farming communities own canals supplying from ten to one hundred ranches. Sometimes but two or three join in taking out water. The uplands are supplied by canals which cost from $10,000 to $80,000. The capital city is provided for by two canals, which send little rivulets through every street and upon every lot in quantities desired by the people. Uncultivated lots and blocks, covered with native sage-brush and bearing all the physical aspects of the desert plains, alternate with lots and blocks upon which water has been applied, where flourish trees and grass, orchards, gardens, and flowers.

The beauty of Boise City, with its wealth of fruit and stately trees, has often been told. Time only adds to its attractiveness. Its annual growth averages 10 per cent in the number and value of its buildings. Idaho was the first of the Territories to provide itself with a permanent capitol building at its own expense, and the people are well satisfied with their investment. The building and furnishing cost about $85,000.

West of the capitol is the immense public school building, and on the east is the court-house, both the best public buildings of their kind yet erected in the State. Occupying another block is the United States assay offices, a solid stone building, erected several years ago at the expense of the United States Government. There is still needed a suitable building for the postoffice, with rooms required for the enlarging business of the United States land offices. The United States marshal has quarters at the court-house. A suitable Government building could be erected on one of our main business thoroughfares, adapted to the needs of the postal service and the land department, for about $40,000, and an appropriation for this purpose should be made at an early day. Other towns in Ada county should not pass unnoticed. The town of Caldwell justly claims an honorable mention on account of its extended wholesale and retail trade, its excellent public and private buildings, and the energy with which its thoughtful people push its interests in every direction. Payette is a beautiful village, drawing its support from both agricultural and lumber interests, while Emmett is the busiest of lumber towns.

The statistics of live-stock and agricultural products elsewhere given are the best evidence of the strength and varied nature of the resources of Ada county. In the yield of fruit and vegetables Ada county ranks first in the State; in hay it ranks second; in grain it stands third. Perhaps the time is not far distant when Ada will rank first in all these particulars, since the real development of the county has but fairly commenced.

The year 1890 was one of remarkable prosperity for Ada county. More than 10,000 acres were added to its area of cultivated lands; the amount of capital invested in agriculture increased 26 per cent; to the extent of its irrigating canals there was added 30 per cent. Turning from agriculture to trade, we find the increase in ordinary traffic has been 25 per cent; the increase in new buildings over the growth of last year has been 50 per cent; and the increase in railway traffic has been 100 per cent. From three railway stations the export of wool has been 793,907 pounds. The number of sheep kept in Ada county was increased 15 per cent during the past year.

Looking forward the outlook is brighter still. Two million dollars will, during the coming year, be invested in irrigating canals, enabling farming operations to increase 20 per cent. Building is likely to be limited simply to the supply of material. Government lands are entered as fast as irrigating canals are surveyed by responsible companies, settlers valuing the lands so highly that they are willing to wait any reasonable time for the actual construction of canals. One year ago lands on the plains, contiguous to water supply, with very limited improvements, for which Government title had been secured, were quoted generally at $10 per acre. Now these lands rarely sell below $20 per acre. These prices are justified by the prices which their products bring. The following were the lowest wholesale quotations of Ada county products on October.3, 1890.

| | | |
|---|---|---|
| Wheat flour | per 100 pounds | $ 2 25 |
| Corn meal | " | 2 25 |
| Wheat | " | 1 16⅝ |
| Oats | " | 1 50 |
| Corn | " | 1 50 |
| Barley | " | 1 35 |
| Rye | " | 1 40 |
| Timothy, loose | per ton | 9 00 |
| Timothy, baled | " | 12 00 |
| Lucerne, loose | " | 8 00 |
| Lucerne, baled | " | 11 00 |
| Clover, loose | " | 8 00 |
| Clover, baled | " | 11 00 |
| Potatoes, Irish | per 100 pounds | 1 50 |
| Dairy butter | per pound | 35 |
| Ranch " | " | 30 |
| Eggs | per dozen | 35 |

It will be very readily seen that the price of hay, the product of which usually reaches four tons to the acre, justified a high value for Ada county lands, in addition to paying the usual irrigation charge for water.

Add to these attractions the fact that the mild and equable climate of Ada county has no superior; that the market for its products is practically unlimited, and that the experiments of the past two years have demonstrated that the soil of the plains is all that can be desired for tree and fruit culture, and one is able to realize what groves, orchards, and gardens will crown this soil, which only three years ago was simply desert and desolation.

More than a quarter million acres in Ada county will yet be redeemed from the desert. The discovery of water in the foot-hills of the Boisé Mountain range opens new prospects in this direction. If the mountains are veined with hidden streams as now seems probable, the development of Ada county will soon produce wealth equal to that heretofore enjoyed by the entire State of Idaho. The gold mines of the Boisé range are attracting more and more attention, and the best practical miners predict the early discovery of richer gold deposits than are yet known in the mountain country.

The towns of Ada county may be separately mentioned as follows:

Boisé City now contains a population of 2,311, and is increasing at the rate of 20 per cent per year. A quarter of a million dollars has been spent in improvements during the last six months. The daily average of the business transactions of its two banks is now $62,000, or a yearly business of $19,344,000. Real estate has advanced more than 100 per cent. Sales of real estate last year were scarcely $5,000 per month; for the six months ending October 1, 1890, the sales amounted to more than $400,000, or $70,000 per month.

The entire city has this year been covered with a spendid water supply system. Eleven miles of water-pipe have been laid, bringing water from artesian wells at the foot of the mountains. The fall is 170 feet, and the pressure enables the fire department to cover the tallest buildings without the use of engines. A sewerage system will be provided in 1891 adequate to the needs of the city.

The daily business of the railway office in 1889 was $500; it has increased in 1890 to $1,100, or $33,000 per month. The lumber and brick business has quadrupled. For six weeks the city was without a lumber supply, so completely were the stocks of the entire county exhausted. There is within forty miles of Boisé City the finest body of timber remaining in Idaho; but it can only be made available and profitably handled by the construction of a railway through Boisé Cañon, and it is hoped that such a railway will be built in the near future, thus insuring this city against a further lumber famine.

Thus the Capital city has kept pace with the wonderful growth of the State of Idaho in every direction. It is growing in mineral resources, in agricultural and horticultural area, in general wealth, in the comforts of life, in population, in trade, and in all else that goes to make a beautiful, healthful, and prosperous city.

CALDWELL AND ITS SURROUNDINGS.—Caldwell is on the Oregon Short Line Railway, 30 miles west of Boisé City, and 447 southeast of Portland, Oregon. Seven years ago the place where Caldwell now stands was an alkali desert, but on the advent of the railroad in 1883 the town was established. Its growth has been rapid. So situated as to be the commercial center of a large stock-growing and agricultural region, it has pushed ahead by the demands of the country until to-day one of the prettiest towns in Idaho marks the spot where but a short time since the sage-brush reigned supreme. As to the location of Caldwell much can be said situated as it is at the foot of the Upper Boisé Valley, and at the head of the Lower Valley. It commands a vast amount of trade from both these fertile districts, which stretch away for miles in either direction. North of the city about a mile is the cañon, through which the Boisé River flows on its way to join the mighty Snake River, to the west and north. At this point the river is crossed by a substantial bridge, at the west end of which the Sebree irrigation canal diverges to the right and flows off across the valley.  On reaching the summit of the range of hills just beyond this bridge, one is struck by the vast panorama of fields, farms, and fertile valleys stretching as far as the eye can see.  Acres upon acres of land tributary to this growing city are as yet uncultivated, and only need the application of water and the muscle of the farmer to turn it into a source of vast revenue both to the tiller and the community at large.  The amount of business transacted at this station is very large, drawing trade as it does for a radius of over 100 miles in every direction.  The volume of business transacted seems impossible when you think of its sparsely-settled country.  A few figures will show the business done at the depot, which is an index to the general business of the community.  For the year 1888 there were 15,178,242 pounds of merchandise received and forwarded.  This does not include live-stock shipments, of which there were 425 cars forwarded.  The cash receipts at the station were $73,106.34.  This is a good record for a town of 500 people (which was the population at that time), of paying over $200 per day the year round for freight.  In 1889 $84,458.86 was paid the railroad company at this station.

Two years ago the population was 432, but to-day it is 779.  The town has three substantial church buildings, a fine brick school house, and several elegant brick business blocks.  The residences are not on the "shack" order, but are neat substantial houses, many of them of the most modern architecture.  The increase of business keeps ahead of the town, with mercantile establishments which carry $100,000 stocks.  The business of the town is rapidly running into wholesale instead of retail.  The leading merchants report an increase of 50 per cent in all lines of business during the past eleven months.

The following buildings have been erected since January 1, 1890:  Six business houses and 18 residences, at an actual cost of $49,750.

The people are enterprising, liberal, and cultured.  Caldwell is indeed further advanced than the average town.  Its railroads are making it an objective point, and it promises to become a railroad as well as an agricultural city.

PAYETTE AND VICINITY.—During the past year Payette and the surrounding country tributary to the town has made a very noticeable growth.  In the town many fine brick buildings have been erected, both for school, business and residence uses; and in the country large barns and good, attractive looking and substantial dwelling houses have been built.  Hundreds of miles of fencing have been put up, and thousands of acres of the rich bottom lands, covered by irrigating canals, have been put in cultivation.  There were raised this year from the lands just about Payette, within a radius of say six miles, 7,000 tons of timothy, clover and alfalfa hay; at least 40,000 bushels of wheat, and many thousand bushels of oats and barley.  Every one who has land in cultivation grows more or less vegetables.  The quality of all kinds of grain and vegetables is strictly first-class, and the quantity of vegetables produced from an acre of irrigated land is very large.  Thousands of heads of cattle, horses and sheep will be fed from the hay raised, and many train loads will also be shipped away to other markets. The country about Payette has made greater development in the way of fruit culture than almost any other part of Idaho. There are here two of the largest nurseries in the Northwest; and principally from these sources have been drawn supplies by the people living in this valley for large orchards and vineyards, and to-day thousands of acres of land are covered with young and thrifty-growing fruit farms, that in the near future will make their owners independent, and will fix a valuation on these lands similar to fruit lands in the fruit-growing districts of California and Oregon. All classes and kinds of prunes, and nearly every kind of apples, pears and grapes have proven a success. The fruit season is very early about Payette; already large shipments have been made to Idaho and Montana points. This industry bids fair to be the leading one with this section in the future. There is in construction in the Payette Valley large irrigating canals that will open for settlement much more land of equally good character as that now under 'cultivation. The amount of business done for the year 1890 will nearly double that of 1889.

The town of Nampa forms the junction of the Oregon Short Line and Idaho Central Railways. It has more than doubled its population and wealth during the past year, having risen from about 225 in 1889, to 500 people in 1890. A fine hotel has been built this year, a commodious school house, and many business buildings and residences.

Emmett is an active lumber and agricultural village, on the Payette River. The farmers of that section are quite prosperous; their farms are in a high state of cultivation, and new ranches are being opened by intelligent settlers.

## ALTURAS COUNTY.

| | Assessment Values. |
|---|---|
| Improved land patented, 14,196 acres | $ 27,214 |
| Improvements on above | 37,870 |
| Improvements on unpatented land, 1,690 acres | 12,680 |
| Improvements on mining claims | 17,250 |
| 4 quartz mills | 26,500 |
| 9 concentrators | 16,750 |
| 2 samplers | 4,300 |
| 2 smelters | 4,800 |
| City and town lots | 85,252 |
| Improvements on lots | 135,315 |
| Mining ditches | 4,027 |
| Money on hand | 6,650 |
| 1,685 cattle at $12.64 | 12,310 |
| Farming utensils | 1,310 |
| Fixtures | 3,885 |
| Furniture | 4,980 |
| Goods, wares and merchandise | 56,375 |
| Harness, robes and saddles | 1,730 |
| 80 hogs at $3.15 | 252 |
| 971 American horses at $30.95 | 30,053 |
| Jewelry and silverware | 210 |
| Lumber | 2,100 |
| 96 mules at $35 | 3,360 |
| Musical instruments | 1,195 |
| 8 oxen at $25 | 200 |
| Sewing-machines | 225 |
| Wagons and vehicles | 8,866 |
| 1,795 cords wood at $2 | 3,590 |
| Bank stock | 10,000 |
| Other personal property | 16,283 |
| Oregon Short Line Railway Company | 101,270 |
| Total valuation | $645,802 |

This county has won wide and lasting fame as a rich mining district. Temporary causes have operated to check its development in this direction, but the fact is well established that the hills and gulches of Alturas county abound in rich mineral veins and ledges; they have made fortunes for many men already, and there are more to develop, sufficient to enrich a regiment of people, and profitably employ thousands more. Prospectors have never abandoned the field, and the results this year are very encouraging.

The county contains three quartz mills, three smelters, and eight concentrators, having a united capacity of 390 tons daily. The ores are classed as lead silver ores, carrying a high percentage of lead, and high grade in silver. Referring to the record kept by a leading assayer of Hailey, the average value of Alturas ores, in lead and silver, basing the value on present quotations, is $160 per ton. Shipments for this year will aggregate 6,000 tons, the ores of this county finding a ready market in Denver, Omaha and Kansas City.

About 1,000,000 feet of lumber, and 100,000 shingles have been cut in five mills and the timber supply is still abundant. This county owns a good court house worth $40,000, and a school house which cost $30,000.

The agricultural development of the county continues, the area of patented lands having increased 60 per cent during the past year. The elevation is such that the farming season is limited; yet the productiveness of the farms is a surprise. The county is well watered, and the irrigation system is annually extended. Rates of wages are remunerative, and the settlers are prosperous. The county commissioners have expended considerable money in roads and bridges, enabling the merchants to command the trade of districts beyond their natural boundaries. Few people have ever met reverses with greater courage, or struggled with larger zeal to overcome obstacles.

Hailey and Ketchum are the principal towns, and both are adorned with public and private buildings in every way creditable to their people.

During the year 1888 several of the most important mines of this county ceased to be productive, and many proclaimed that this district had seen its best days. During the last winter and spring a considerable number left for new fields; but those who understood best the mineral resources of this county remained steadfast in the faith that they were beginning rather than ending the production of the precious metals here. It is now stated that there are fifty mines paying a liberal profit to their owners. While there have been periods in the history of this county when the total output was greater than now, so great a number of profitable mines has never been reached before, and the prospect for a greatly increased yield the coming year is cheering in the highest degree.

The town of Ketchum remains the great distributing point for the vast mining region to the northwest, and one of the principal shipping points for all of Custer county and the districts north and northeast. Many causes have contributed to temporarily retard the growth of the place, yet its citizens have just completed, at heavy expense, a system of water-works unexcelled in the entire State.

The returns given in the table of agricultural products show that Alturas county will not rest its fame upon its mines alone, but that its yield of grain and vegetables is highly creditable. The county ranks high in the business of stock-raising, and excels in the proportion of the better grades.

## BEAR LAKE COUNTY.

|  | Assessment Values. |
|---|---|
| Oregon Short Line Railroad Company | $295,620 |
| Western Union Telegraph Company | 2,733 |
| Deseret Telegraph Company | 300 |
| Improved land patented, 27,330 acres | 100,250 |
| Improvements on above | 100,127 |
| Land unpatented, 18,000 acres | 75,000 |
| Improvements on above | 62,050 |
| Money on hand | 2,150 |
| 8,197 stock cattle | 89,830 |
| Farming utensils | 7,175 |
| Fire-arms | 300 |
| Store fixtures | 3,500 |
| Goods, wares and merchandise | 59,970 |
| Harness, robes and saddles | 3,246 |
| 482 hogs | 1,447 |
| 200 American horses | 12,000 |
| 2,752 Spanish horses | 69,135 |
| Lumber | 2,000 |
| Machinery | 4,215 |
| Musical instruments | 2,800 |
| Pianos | 2,000 |
| Sewing machines | 1,500 |
| 886 sheep at $2 | 1,772 |
| Wagons and vehicles (588) | 13,305 |
| 100 watches at $15 | 1,500 |
| Total valuation | $913,915 |

This county has been settled for about twenty years, the pioneers being colonists of the Mormon Church. The result is seen in a population denser than in any other county of Idaho, and a larger proportion of the soil under cultivation.

A considerable portion of the county is mountainous, and covered with a heavy growth of pine timber. Saw-mills have been diligently cutting away in these forests for half a generation, but the supply is abundant still. The elevation of the county is so great that no fruit is grown, but, on the other hand, water is so abundant that the grain and grass crop is marvelous.

Under a system early adopted the residents of the villages each have a small acreage near by. The necessities of life are therefore at the easy command of all, each family being able to employ its own members, and abject poverty rendered impossible. Close neighborhoods, a comfortable social life, and a heavy population within a small system, while few enjoy great wealth.

Bear Lake, from which the county takes its name, is a large body of water, well stocked with fish, and is a natural reservoir for an immense section. Should a system of storage reservoirs be adopted by the Federal Government, Bear Lake county will be the seat of the beginnings of this great project, and a large expenditure of public money among its people would result.

The Oregon Short Line traverses this county, and at Montpelier a large number of railway employes have their homes. Both Paris and Montpelier are handsome and prosperous towns, and reasonably well provided with educational facilities. Paris is the county seat, and it has a good courthouse and a large Mormon tabernacle. Population 893.

In the present condition of the State laws this population of over six thousand persons contains but about two hundred and fifty legal voters. The bulk of the people are Mormons, who are disfranchised not as a church, but as an association practicing or teaching polygamy.

The main railroad business of this county is transacted at Montpelier. Population 1,174. The town constitutes a railway freight division, and many railway employes are building permanent homes in this beautiful village. They are a thrifty and intelligent class of citizens. It is probable that the railway company will greatly enlarge its shops and enginehouse at this point; a newspaper has been recently established and the educational facilities of the place improved.

## BINGHAM COUNTY.

|  | Assessment Values. |
|---|---:|
| Utah and Northern Railway Company | $1,119,630 |
| Oregon Short Line Railway Company | 379,015 |
| Improved land patented, 117,148 acres | 325,434 |
| Improvements on above | 107,252 |
| Improvements on unpatented land | 101,343 |
| Western Union Telegraph Company | 25,306 |
| Town lots | 43,615 |
| Improvements on same | 213,110 |
| Money on hand | 10,000 |
| 19,706 stock cattle at $11.62 | 229,118 |
| 2,400 American cows at $15 | 36,000 |
| Farming utensils | 16,304 |
| Store fixtures | 5,000 |
| Furniture | 5,300 |
| Goods, wares and merchandise | 204,625 |
| 591 hogs | 2,616 |
| Six thoroughbred horses at $300 | 1,800 |
| 27 graded horses at $100 | 2,700 |
| 8,369 American horses | 223,482 |
| Jacks and jennies | 150 |
| Machinery | 35,550 |
| 100 mules at $40 | 4,000 |
| 15 pianos | 3,000 |
| 100 sewing machines | 1,500 |
| 7,332 sheep | 10,355 |
| 1,457 wagons and vehicles | 34,872 |
| Bank stock | 14,400 |
| Other personal property | 22,181 |
| Total valuation | $3,177,658 |

The county of Bingham covers 165 miles from north to south and 88 miles from east to west. It ranks first in population among the counties of Idaho, and second in taxable wealth. It embraces within its limits a variety of soil, climate, scenery, employments and products equal to any other. It is an empire in extent and possibilities; it is a State in its resources and capacities. To write of it or describe it is a task which should have the help of many minds and months of time. Neither of these are at our service, and this inadequate review can only show our good will; it cannot do justice to the county or its people.

A rapid description will naturally look upon the county in triplicate— its southeast, or great mineral and grazing belt; its center, or chief agricultural section; its vast north, with its great forests, its unrivaled natural scenery, and its multitudinous farms. The population of this county may be roughly guessed or estimated; the actual number which, within the last three years, have flocked into its valleys and spread over its plains will not be known till the patient census-taker seeks them out.

Southeast Bingham has for its central business point the town of Soda Springs. This is a city of hotels; the cool resort of health seekers; the center of the most valuable, the most curious, the rarest group of mineral springs known to geographical lore. It is also the center of a body of grazing and agricultural lands, which is winning the attention of thousands of home-seekers, and where the settlers are solidly prosperous. To the north is the Carriboo placer mining district. In its wild fastnesses many shrewd miners are exploring, and if half is true which is told by prospectors there is untold wealth awaiting capitalists of courage and knowledge, who will use both in this wonderful region.

Swinging westward and northward, the towns of Pocatello and Blackfoot are reached. Two years ago there were at Pocatello possibly 200 persons; one year ago there were 500; at this date estimates vary from 1,500 to 2,500. Here are located the most extensive car-shops between Omaha and the Pacific coast, and around the town are grazing lands, rapid streams, and hills tempting to the hunter and prospector. Where so recently but a handful of railroad employés held possession, there is now a national bank, an excellent newspaper, mammoth general stores, good hotels, churches, schools, and all the smaller trades and shops usually accompanying the march of civilization. Just north of Pocatello, and beyond the Indian reservation, is Blackfoot, the county seat. Here is a well-built and well-furnished county court-house; here is the Idaho insane asylum; the United States land offices; a private bank; several business houses and comfortable dwellings; a good school-house, and two substantial brick churches; and from the railway depot there load and depart daily great wagon trains of freight for the mining districts of central Idaho. Within a radius of 20 miles of Blackfoot hundreds of farmers are cultivating valuable ranches, supplied by water from costly canals, where five years ago the coyote was the only live stock and sage-brush the only vegetation.

Twenty-five miles northward is the town of Eagle Rock. Here, in a great stone building, is said to be the largest retail merchandise store in Idaho; here is being built a flouring-mill with the latest improved machinery; here is a bank; a valuable system of city water-works, and about twenty-five firms engaged in various branches of industry. Eagle Rock claims also to rank first in the State in the number of agricultural implements sold. From this point the Union Pacific Railway is expected to extend a branch line along the Snake River, in a northeast course to the National Park, reaching on its course the settlements at Rexburg, Menan, Egin, St. Anthony, and other points, where the growth is already marvelous, and where the increase in population shows no signs of abatement.

Northward still is the village of Camas, an important shipping point for the southern portion of Lemhi county; and still further north is Beaver Cañon, which for six years has held first rank in the manufacture and shipment of lumber. Near each of these towns are abundant streams which nourish the numerous farms. Of all the counties dependent upon irrigation, none excels Bingham in the number and importance of the running streams, and in none is the general system of irrigation surpassed. For three successive years the assessment roll of Bingham county has grown at the rate of $300,000 per annum; and this great increase still continues.

The railway properties, which form fifty per cent of the assessable resources of the county, are valued the same as last year. The increase of more than $300,000, therefore, falls upon the property of private citizens. An actual advance in the local wealth of fully thirty per cent appears. Nearly all of this growth is among the farmers. The amount of improved lands patented has advanced from 75,482 acres in 1889 to 117,148 acres in 1890. A very large number of new farms have been opened, and improvements of the most permanent and valuable character have been made. The system of irrigation, which is more extensively developed in Bingham than in any other county in Idaho, has been still further perfected this year. The county authorities have exercised an enlightened liberality in the construction of bridges and improvement of highways. In the northeastern portion of the county, where new settlements are the more numerous, the increase in the general wealth has attracted the attention of railway authorities, and the early construction of a railway through this region, as a branch of the Utah Northern Line, is looked upon as an assured fact. The prosperity of agriculture has diverted attention, to some extent, from the mining resources of the county, and even the inhabitants of the town are making liberal investments in ranch lands. It is believed that there is sufficient water supply existing in Bingham county to add 100 per cent to the present area of its farm land. The population could be easily doubled outside of the towns, and outside of the timber and mining land. There is still an inexhaustible supply of timber, but somewhat remote from the railroad.

The towns and cities of Bingham county enjoyed a very substantial growth in 1890. The needs of social and business life have both been better provided for through the erection of additionul warehouses, hotels, school houses, etc.

The attention of placer mining experts is still frequently directed to the sands of Snake River, in the endeavor to solve the problem of extracting the fine "flour gold." It has been frequently asserted that the sands of Snake River contain gold enough to pay the national debt, and of this kind of wealth Bingham county has a large proportion.

## BOISE COUNTY.

Assessment Values.

| | |
|---|---|
| Improved land patented, 10,701 acres, value | $39,725 |
| Improvements on above | 39,450 |
| Improvements on unpatented land | 25,395 |
| Improvements on mining claims | 11,000 |
| 10 quartz mills | 50,200 |
| 125 mining ditches | 51,360 |
| 10 irrigating ditches | 1,100 |
| Mortgages | 43,192 |
| Money on hand | 8,283 |
| Brandies and liquors | 3,995 |
| Notes and accounts | 23,312 |
| 2,329 calves, at $10 | 23,290 |
| 222 beef cattle at $25 | 5,550 |
| 5,064 stock cattle, at $14 | 70,896 |
| 47 colts, at $15 | 705 |
| 543 American cows, at $25 | 13,575 |
| Store fixtures | 750 |
| Furniture | 5,300 |
| Goods, wares and merchandise | 55,925 |
| Harness, robes and saddles | 3,313 |
| 712 hogs, at $4 | 2,848 |
| Merchandise | 6,124 |
| 14 thoroughbred horses | 2,000 |
| 2,133 American horses | 62,350 |
| 108,000 feet of lumber | 1,055 |
| Saw-logs | 11,357 |
| Machinery | 4,870 |
| 75 mules | 3,410 |
| 25 musical instruments | 1,305 |
| 32 oxen | 865 |
| 15 pianos | 3,600 |
| Quicksilver | 1,600 |
| 62 sewing machines | 743 |
| 3,927 sheep, at $2 | 7,854 |
| 307 vehicles | 11,175 |
| Watches and jewelry | 2,705 |
| 19,733 cords wood | 14,819 |
| Other personal property | 69,385 |
| **Total valuation** | **$684,381** |

Boise Basin was discovered in 1862 by prospectors, and settlement was stimulated by gold mining. The boundaries of Boise county were established at the first session of the Territorial Legislature, held at Lewiston, and approved February 4, 1864.

By far the largest part of the county is mountainous, and forms part of the greatest and best timbered section of country situated between the Rocky Mountain range and the Blue Mountains of Oregon. A large and prosperous logging business is transacted, with indications of a more important future. The most accessible parts are on Moore's Creek, and the waters of the South, Middle, and North Forks of the Payette River, from which last place the logs are driven to mills on the Lower Payette and the Snake Rivers. Should a railroad be constructed by which lumber could be easily got out of the country the business would become a large one. Preliminary surveys having this object in view have already been made. Many of the saw-mills in the mines were constructed and are run by the owners as adjuncts to their mining claims. One mill is also joined in a bed-rock fluming enterprise. Should an additional supply of water be brought in that would enable continuous working it would undoubtedly be a well paying venture.

The agricultural resources of the county outside of the mountains are the settlements of the Lower Valley and Squaw Creek, and are places adapted to the production of varieties of grain, roots, vegetables, as well as a diversity of fruits, the last two finding their principal market in the mines at good prices. Hay is also put up in large quantities. Much attention is given to stock from the convenient facilities afforded for grazing, and it is notable through the county that much care is given to improved breeding of both horses and cattle. Sheep are well graded up, the average fleece weighing 7 pounds. This year's clip found a market at 14 cents per pound.

Garden Valley, located at the junction of the middle and south branches of the Payette, is the granary of the country. All farming products are cultivated and considerable attention is given to hardy varieties of fruit. Here is established a grist-mill with a capacity of 24 barrels per day. It has for a long time been the principal source of supply for the home market for large quantities of hay, grain and vegetables. Laborers on farms receive from $30 to $40 per month.

Fifteen miles from Garden Valley and on the North Fork, inclosed on all sides with mountains heavily timbered with pine, is Long Valley, a grassy plain stretching north 60 miles with a breadth of 9. It is divided lengthwise by the river, receiving several tributaries in its traverse, which gives fine facilities for, and renders irrigation easy for, a large portion of its area. A short dam placed across the river where it emerges from a lake at the upper end of the valley would afford a storage of water of unlimited quantity.

It is of recent settlement and now has a population estimated at 1,300. Some ditching has been done and quite extensive fencing. Grain and vegetables are cultivated and fruit trees planted. Attention is given principally to stock, both cattle and horses; grazing is unsurpassed, but feed has to be provided for winter. Seven thousand tons of native hay have been put up for that purpose this season. Two saw-mills are steadily employed furnishing lumber. On the tributary streams mines are worked for gold, and a vein of coal discovered this summer on Gold Fork is stated to have a thickness of 7 feet. The waters are abundantly supplied with fine fish, and the genus trout is represented by four varieties.

Mining has always been the largest source of revenue. In early days, ground easily worked—creeks and low bars—first engaged attention, and only heavy diggings remain. Several of the lesser outside camps help to swell the sum total. The mining camp, Dead Wood Basin, is located on a branch of the South Payette. It has a large placer mine, which is worked on an extensive scale, besides several smaller ones. Ledges prospecting well in gold and silver have been located, and considerable work in the way of development has been expended upon them, and, with the construction of a wagon road to facilitate the transportation of machinery and heavy materials, will no doubt become prominent.

The Elmira Silver Mining Company, at Banner, is exclusively a silver producer. It has been worked for several years and with a continually augmenting output, and is now known as one of the most prominent and best paying properties.

The Washington mine is now running with a 20-stamp mill on high-grade ores, carrying both gold and silver. The property is a valuable one, and has a large amount of ore ready for extraction.

The Elk Horn has been known as a great producer; was worked at an early period, and is now crushing good ores. Having a water-power mill, expenses are of course light. A contract has been let to drive a tunnel for deeper development, which will occupy the coming winter.

The Gold Hill Gold and Silver Mining Company, at Quartzburg, is one of long standing, and their property is noted as a continuous running and regular paying mine. The only stoppage for more than twenty years was accidental, and caused by burning of the mill. The workings have reached the depth of 400 feet, but they have for some time and now are taking out ore from the 180-foot level, which presents a face of 40 feet. The mill is of 25-stamp capacity, with automatic feeders, crushers, and automatic air-compressor.

The Queen of the West is located 3 miles from Pioneer. The ore is free milling and easily extracted. The mine is developed by a shaft 172 feet deep and connecting with a tunnel measuring 360 feet. A mill of 20 stamps with capacity for more, and to be run by water power, is near completion. The property is owned by an Eastern company.

The Basin, drained by Moore's Creek, is an area or cluster of placer mines measuring 15 miles either way, and contains the towns of Quartzburg, Granite Creek, Placerville, Centerville, Pioneer, and Idaho City. It has for a long time been noted for its large number of paying placer mines, and from the fact that water has never been in proportion to the ground workable, much gold remains to be taken out, and with an average fall of snow to supply the streams with their usual amount of water, the quantity yearly may be estimated with almost mathematical accuracy.

The county of Boise is one of the best timbered counties in the State and contributes most of the supply of wood and timber to the adjoining county of Ada. This with the necessary consumption of the mines is a heavy draft upon the forests of the county, but worst of all vast forest fires have raged for weeks, despite the utmost efforts of the people to stay them. Vast quantities of timber have been killed, large quantities of cordwood burned, and valuable mining and farming properties imperiled. It is well worth the attention of the General Government, as well as of the local governments, to use all means practicable to stay the frequent occurrence of these fires, as their oft repetition is certain to produce disastrous climatic changes. Once these forests are destroyed the fall of snow and rain is more or less affected, and if not materially lessened passes off in floods in the early season, and leaves those dependent on water for mining and irrigation later in the season destitute.

## CASSIA COUNTY.

| | Assessment Values. |
|---|---:|
| Improved land patented, 48,224 acres | $ 153,710 |
| Improvements on the above | 52,405 |
| Improvements on unpatented land | 34,660 |
| Mining claims | 9,800 |
| Town lots | 5,595 |
| Improvements on the same | 15,440 |
| Irrigating ditches | 3,528 |
| 120 calves | 803 |
| 13,806 stock cattle | 151,866 |
| 47 thoroughbred cows | 1,750 |
| 635 American cows | 12,700 |
| 72 graded cows | 1,355 |
| Fixtures | 225 |
| Furniture | 650 |
| Goods, wares and merchandise | 18,605 |
| Harness, robes and saddles | 2,292 |
| 399 hogs | 1,700 |
| 12 thoroughbred horses | 3,050 |
| 50 colts | 460 |
| 731 American horses | 36,042 |
| 4,078 Spanish horses | 73,127 |
| Jacks | 150 |
| Machinery | 7,430 |
| 72 mules | 2,215 |
| 7 oxen | 200 |
| 18 pianos and organs | 610 |
| 25,850 sheep | 51,700 |
| Solvent credits | 7,200 |
| 483 wagons | 15,865 |
| 9 watches | 330 |
| Grist and saw mills | 6,500 |
| Ferry-boats | 650 |
| Total valuation | $672,613 |

From the earliest settlement of this county its growth has been steady and uniform. Its irrigating canals have been planned, built and extended by far-sighted pioneers. Year by year the acreage of improved land redeemed from the desert by water conducted from distant springs and streams has been largely increased, and the refreshed and invigorated soil has made abundant return to the farmer. Still, more than 1,000,000 acres wait for like relief. In no part of the State is the extension of the reservoir and canal system, under the direction of the United States Government, more largely watched or more ardently desired than in Cassia, for this extension and development cannot fail to place this county in the front rank of population and wealth.

Attempts have been made, in a desultory way, to develop the mineral resources of this county, and indications of gold, silver, lead and other deposits are found all over the mountains. Assays are frequently made running away up into the thousands, but work has not been prosecuted to any depth, and there is no reliable information as to what may be lying underneath. The county will certainly justify extensive and thorough prospecting, for these numerous rich spurs must certainly lead to one or more great central deposits.

Placer mines are the most promising for immediate results. This county has a frontage on Snake River of over 200 miles, and the sands of this stream are rich in gold through its entire length. Sanguine miners state that with abundant water, having sufficient head and properly worked, there would be enough taken out of these deposits to pay the national debt.

While this statement is doubtless extravagant, still there is foundation for large estimates.

This county also contains extensive deposits of the very best fire-proof mineral paint, large deposits of fine marble, sandstone, granite, mica and many indications of abundance of coal.

There is a fair and steady demand for intelligent labor among the ranch and stock men. Reliable herders receive $35 to $40 per month; farm hands, $25 to $30 per month; during haying $2 per day is paid.

Very little can be added to the previous reports concerning this county, and a large growth can hardly be looked for before the advent of railways. The inducements offered to capitalists and settlers are very attractive. The topographical features of the county and the quality of the soil, together with the abundance of water in Snake River, invite large irrigation projects which require immense capital. Should private enterprise fail to take up the great work of supplying the northern portion of Cassia county with irrigation, it is probable that the aid of the National Government will be invoked in a need so great and a situation so meritorious.

The valleys of the central and western portions of this county are fairly supplied with water, and the settlers are constantly extending their local irrigation systems. There is therefore a constant annual increase in the acreage of cultivated lands, and many prosperous homes will yet be established in Cassia. The county is well supplied with timber for fuel and for building purposes.

A railway line has been surveyed from Salt Lake City, through Cassia, to connect the capital of Utah with the towns and cities of southern Idaho. Such a line if built would double the population and business of Cassia county, and would receive from the day of its opening a living patronage. The attention of railway authorities is invited to this project, as one promising excellent results.

In spite of all obstacles the industrious people of Cassia have prospered during 1890. The towns of Albion and Oakley are creditably located and built. The county affairs are economically handled. The exports of this county, though exchanged under most unfavorable conditions, are quite large. The climate is moderate and healthful. New settlers will find good locations and fair water supply awaiting development; they will find peace-loving communities, and public sentiment growing in intelligence and enterprise.

## CUSTER COUNTY.

Assessment Values.

| | |
|---|---|
| Land, 25,780 acres, improvements | $196,290 |
| 8 quartz mills | 45,000 |
| 3 concentrators | 18,000 |
| 3 smelters | 17,000 |
| Mining ditches | 4,200 |
| Irrigation ditches | 8,430 |
| State and county bonds | 17,460 |
| Money on hand | 15,530 |
| 490 beef cattle at $25 | 12,250 |
| 7,685 stock cattle at $12 | 92,220 |
| 45 thoroughbred cows at $40 | 1,800 |

Assessment Values.

| | |
|---|---:|
| 88 American cows at $25 | $ 2,200 |
| Farming utensils | 6,840 |
| Store and saloon fixtures | 10,490 |
| Furniture | 8,640 |
| Goods, wares and merchandise | 108,450 |
| 240 hogs | 1,920 |
| 5 graded horses at $400 | 2,000 |
| 210 American horses at $70 | 14,700 |
| 2,984 mixed horses at $25 | 74,600 |
| 290 mules at $40 | 11,600 |
| 45 musical instruments at $60 | 2,700 |
| 115 sewing machines at $20 | 2,300 |
| Solvent credits | 15,450 |
| 550 vehicles at $40 | 1,800 |
| 100 watches at $40 | 4,000 |
| 18,350 sheep at $1.50 | 27,800 |
| Total valuation | $723,670 |

Custer county was organized by act of the Legislature passed on the 8th day of January, 1881, which went into effect on the 1st day of April of the same year. The territory of which it is composed was taken from Lemhi and Alturas counties. The enumeration made at the late census places its population at 2,174. This does not represent the real number of inhabitants within its borders. Many of the people are remote from settlements engaged in prospecting, others with flocks and herds scattered over a territory as large as the State of Connecticut. The county contains approximately 4,350 square miles. Of this, the greater part is mountainous, containing many mining districts, though there are three large agricultural valleys, besides smaller tracts, where all the cereals and vegetables common to this climate are grown. The greater tracts alluded to are Lost River, Pah Samari and Round Valley.

### MINERAL RESOURCES.

Mining is at present and for many years will be the leading industry of the county. There are more than two hundred developed and productive quartz-mining properties within its limits, besides over two thousand prospects, a large number of which will undoubtedly prove to be rich mines.

The mineral belt crossing the western portion of Custer county is one of the most extensive in the West. It is at least 100 miles in length and 50 in width, interspersed with gold and silver ores along its entire extent. This section of the county is not well provided with roads, and the ores have been freighted to the railroad at Ketchum on pack animals. With all this attendant expense they have paid. It will be seen from this fact that great returns will be made to the mine-owners when better means of transportation shall be afforded or the ores can be reduced in the vicinity of the mines.

The most prominent among the mining districts of Custer county are Lost River, on the stage road from Blackfoot to Challis, about 50 miles south of the latter; Yankee Fork, 35 miles west of Challis; Bay Horse, 12 miles southwest of Challis; Kinnikinnick, 16 miles south of Bay Horse; Squaw Creek, 4 miles farther south, and East Fork, 35 miles.

YANKEE FORK MINING DISTRICT.—The mines of this district have been very productive of both gold and silver, and have been considered the best in the country. The principal among them are the Unknown, Charles Dickens, Grand Prize, Grey Eagle, Lucky Boy, Badger, Summit, Continental, Fourth of July, Daniel O'Connell, Juliet, Montana, Whale, Wayne and Anna. A 30-stamp mill erected in 1880, the capacity of which was greatly enlarged in 1882, has crushed many thousand tons of ore, and added several millions of dollars to the gold and silver output of Idaho. There is but little lead in the ores of this district. .

EAST FORK OR GERMANIA BASIN.—The mines in this district are in a brown porphyry formation with true fissure veins, and have produced $100 in silver and $20 in gold to the ton of ore. The Crœsus, Bible Back, Idaho, Tyrolese, Jefferson, Washington, Stutterberg and Sperling are all producing both gold and silver.

BAY HORSE DISTRICT.—The Ramshorn group of mines in this district have been extensive producers of silver. The Ramshorn, Utah Boy, Post Boy and Montreal are among the oldest discoveries in the county, The Beardsley, Excelsior, Hood, Good Enough, Keno, Jarvis, Barton, Homestake, Dumpby, Riverview, Hoosier, Sky Lark, Silver Wing, Utah Boy and Post Boy carry high grade ores. Some of these mines carry a large percentage of lead, iron and silica. The last named minerals perform an important part in the formation of fluxes for smelting. There is a 40-ton smelter in the district situated upon Bay Horse creek. Charcoal is used for fuel.

KINNIKINNICK DISTRICT.—At the town of Clayton, in this district, a smelter is in operation, and makes large shipments of bullion to Ketchum. It is doing a fine business. Among the mines owned by the company are the Ella, Overland, Faithful Boy and Monitor. The Silver Bill, You Know and Redemption are all valuable mines.

There are many good mines in Squaw Creek, Slate Creek, and neighboring districts. They carry a fair percentage of lead and sixty ounces of silver to the ton. Teams loaded with bullion, the silver of which is mostly the product of these mines, are constantly upon the road from Clayton to Ketchum at all seasons except for a time in winter when the intervening mountains are impassable from the depth of snow.

LOST RIVER DISTRICT.—This mining district has several valuable properties containing, lead, silver, and copper ores. The Grand Prize, Alice, Mammoth, Black Daisy, Jay Gould, Buena Vista, Golden Wave, Copper King, Henrietta and Old Judge are the most prominent.

One of the greatest difficulties in the way of the development of the mines of Custer county has been in their isolation and transportation being so great. In view of the richness of the mines, the great agricultural capabilities of the county, the fact that one-fourth of its mountainous area is heavily timbered with spruce, fir and pine, must all combine to render railroad facilities for its people an event of the near future. A branch road connecting with the Utah and Northern or with the Union Pacific, or both, would be an enterprise attended with profitable results.

## AGRICULTURE.

If Custer county excels as a mining section, it none the less can lay claim to excellence as a farming and stock-raising district. It has several valleys suitable for such purpose, chief among which are those of Lost River, Pah Samari and Round Valley.

The Lost River Valley contains therein about 100 square miles of tillable land, the Pah Samari about fifty, and Round Valley about thirty. The time is not far distant when every acre of it will be made available for farming purposes. The business of the agriculturist has been made profitable because he has been able to find a home market. The number of consumers of farm productions will increase as fast as the agricultural population.

Until within the past six years fruit culture has been entirely neglected. Within that time large numbers of apple, plum, pear and cherry trees have been planted in the various valleys, notably the Round Valley, where they are flourishing. There is no doubt but that in a few years all the fruit will be raised in this county that the wants of the people require. Wild berries are very abundant.

Stock Raising.—There are thousands of acres of excellent grazing lands, not only in the valleys but upon the mountain sides. Experience has demonstrated, however, that it is well for the stock man to be prepared to meet possibilities of severe winters.

Timber.—There are many tracts of fine timber in Custer county. Millions of feet might be exported and enough left to provide for the wants of its inhabitants for mining, building, farming, and domestic purposes with all of its prospective population for an indefinite period of time.

There is but little surveyed land in the county, and until the past year there has been none. Many of the farmers have lived on their claims for periods of ten years and are subject to great hardship, not knowing where their boundaries will be when the land is surveyed, and being unable to obtain title whereby transfer of any portion can be made.

## ELMORE COUNTY.

|  | Assessment Values. |
|---|---|
| Improved land patented, 16,145 acres | $ 49,616 |
| Improvements on above | 38,560 |
| Improvements on unpatented land, 4,215 acres | 9,825 |
| 31 mining claims | 7,661 |
| Telegraph lines | 5,876 |
| 13 quartz mills | 141,471 |
| 1 concentrator | 250 |
| 8 mining ditches | 5,996 |
| 14 irrigating ditches | 370 |
| Oregon Short Line Railway Company | 420,355 |
| Money on hand | 21,050 |
| 4,597 stock cattle | 53,765 |
| Farming utensils | 1,510 |
| Fire-arms | 80 |
| Harness, robes and saddles | 15,221 |
| 73 hogs | 375 |
| Goods, wares and merchandise | 36,970 |
| 1,860 American horses | 50,083 |
| Machinery | 141,810 |
| Pianos and organs | 1,340 |
| 49 sewing-machines | 925 |
| 25,615 sheep | 51,230 |
| 176 vehicles | 6,660 |
| 38 watches | 907 |
| Wood | 5,000 |
| Improvements on town lots | 113,000 |
| Total valuation | 1,179,906 |

The sources of wealth in Elmore county are fourfold; quartz mining, placer mining, forestry, and stock raising. Near the northern boundary of this county is the town of Atlanta, the oldest quartz mining town of southern Idaho. Twenty years ago, unusually large investments of capital in machinery and mining development were made at this place, and for a time the output of gold was enormous. Why these great mines have remained unopened for half a generation is not known to the public. Disagreement and litigation among the owners are said to be part of the causes of this unfortunate state of affairs. The place is also quite difficult of access, and mining operations here require very large capital. The best informed believe that the time is not far distant when the famous mines of Atlanta will reopen their treasures.

Sixteen miles to the south of Atlanta and 60 miles north of Mountain Home is Rocky Bar, the present county seat. At or near this place about twenty mines are in course of development. Expensive mills and machinery have been introduced, and strong companies control the field. During the year 1888, the yield of gold reached over half a million dollars.

Heretofore the profits of mining have drawn attention away from stock-raising and farming; irrigating canals have not been constructed to an extent equal to other counties, but public attention is now awakened in this direction. Shipments from Mountain Home show conclusively that the production of live stock and transactions in wool, hides and grain are rapidly increasing. Many irrigating ditches are assuming the proportions of extensive canals, the older farmers are finding to their own gratification that orchards can be successfuly cultivated. Indeed this is an era of wise beginnings of great enterprises in Elmore county.

The great pine forests of this county have as yet been lightly touched by the hand of man. Local needs have kept six saw-mills in operation and about 1,000,000 feet of lumber have been manufactured. When the county government shall be able to greatly improve the highways this industry will be rapidly developed. The towns of Rocky Bar, Mountain Home, and Glenn's Ferry are improving in all directions. The latter town is a railroad-division, with railway shops and engine-houses. Both public and private buildings in each of these towns are increasing in number and value, and the educational system is being developed. Few counties in Idaho offer greater inducements to new settlers at this time.

The number of acres of patented lands in Elmore county increased 60 per cent during 1890 and the improvements on the ranch lands have been of a permanent and valuable character. This county needs a careful survey by a civil engineer to ascertain definitely its levels. There are many streams carrying a heavy body of water, sufficient to irrigate thousands of acres, but private enterprise has not been able as yet to devise a complete system of canals. The supply of water so far controlled has been utilized in the improvements of many farms of exceeding beauty and productiveness, but their entire area is not equal to one-tenth of the good soil of this county. Meanwhile the attention of capitalists is directed to this county, and definite information can be obtained by addressing the president of the board of trade, Mountain Home.

The county seat for nearly two years was temporarily located at Rocky Bar, a mining town of thrift and energy, but the votes of the people have decided that the permanent location of the county's capital shall hereafter be at Mountain Home, a point on the Oregon Short Line, more convenient to the majority of the people.

Mountain Home has about 600 inhabitants and is a substantial, handsome, and well-built town. It is the leading shipping point for a broad district of country and the railroad and general merchandise business here is large. It is one of the most important wool shipping points in Idaho, and if a proper water supply is obtained should be the seat of great woolen manufactures.

The county will provide substantial buildings at Mountain Home during the coming year.

Glenn's Ferry is an active railroad town, which during the last two years has grown from nothing to a population only second to Mountain Home. It is a freight division of the Oregon Short Line, and many railway employes have their homes here. The title to the lands upon which it stands has recently been permanently settled, and we now look for the erection of valuable stores and tasteful residences. That the town and county are prosperous is evidenced by the rates of wages paid, which are authoritatively quoted as follows: Locomotive engineers and conductors, $3.85 per 100 miles; firemen and brakemen, $2.25 per 100 miles; stationary engineers, $75 per month; machinists, $3.50 per day; boiler-makers, $3.50 per day; blacksmiths and carpenters, $3 to $3.50 per day; painters, $2.75 per day; laborers, $2 per day; hostlers, $75 per month; track foremen, $65 per month; track laborers, $1.65 per day; agents and operators, $75 to $90 per month; ranch hands, $30 per month and board; placer miners, $2 per day and board; herders, $50 per month and board.

### MINING INTERESTS OF ELMORE COUNTY.

The Alturas Company, of Rocky Bar, have been sinking a large treble compartment shaft for the past six months, expending in such labor the sum of $50,000. The work is now nearly complete, and when it is, will give employment to at least one hundred and fifty men.

The Mountain Goat Company have been developing their mine for the past year, and are now erecting new hoisting and pumping works which will be completed in the near future, and when so completed will give employment to not less than sixty men. The Comfort Consolidated Company have also been at work nearly the entire year in sinking a large treble compartment shaft, erecting a new 20-stamp mill, new hoisting and pumping works, etc., and when this is completed, which will be in a few weeks, will furnish employment to not less than one hundred men.

The White Star Company is now erecting a mill of 50 tons capacity per day, and will have it completed this autumn. This mill is being erected upon the Dividend mine, adjacent to the South Boise River, and when completed will give employment to not less than sixty men. There are a large number of mines owned by private individuals who are extracting goodly quantities of ore of an excellent grade. These mines are scattered all over this district, and the ore extracted from them is reduced in two custom mills, yielding in almost every instance generous returns to the owners, and sufficient to enable such owners to support their families and themselves and also to educate their children, in most instances far above the average of working people. The happy surroundings of their homes would indicate comfort and prosperity.

There are in Rocky Bar district 122 head of stamps with a crushing capacity of 224 tons of ore daily. Then the White Star Company (Griffin mill), with a capacity of 50 tons daily, makes the total of crushing and reducing capacity of the camp 274 tons. On the Red Warrior is located the Wide West Company's mill. This company has been closed down for the past season, owing to some misunderstanding among the owners. The same may be said of the Bonapart Company. Both of these companies will recommence operations in a short time and will give employment to not less than one hundred and fifty men, and add very largely to the output and prosperity of the county.

ATLANTA DISTRICT.—There are in this district five mills, consisting of 75 head of stamps, with a crushing and reducing capacity of 150 tons daily. From various causes this camp has for some time been under a cloud. The chief cause, however, is that some of the principal mines were bonded to an English syndicate for sale for the sum of $600,000, and the sale was at one time effected, but owing to the Alien land law the principal promoters refused to endorse the sale until such law could be repealed, so far as relating to mines and mining locations. Now that Idaho is a State, this sale will doubtless be consummated within the next three months and will give employment as formerly to not less than four hundred men.

There is also in Atlanta two concentrating mills, which have a daily capacity of 40 tons, both of which are now in constant operation and producing marvelous results upon ores, which were hitherto considered worthless and thrown over the various dumps.

PINE GROVE DISTRICT.—This district can boast of some remarkably rich mines, both as to quantity and quality of ore. They have one ten-stamp mill, which is in constant operation, producing results which are entirely satisfactory to the owners, and causing an anxious inquiry among mining men. Indeed, when the development work now under way shall have been completed, a boom must in the natural course of business be inaugurated. The location of this camp is peculiarly adapted to entice population within its borders. Here we find "Therman Springs," with a temperature the year round from 50° to 150° Fahrenheit, and possessing medicinal properties of remarkable efficacy, and particuiarly so in the case of rheumatism and chronic diseases. It is surrounded by beautiful groves of primeval forests and fertile grazing lands, bountifully watered, and capable of sustaining a population of many thousands.

## IDAHO COUNTY.

|  | Assessment Values. |
|---|---|
| Improved land patented, 61,236 acres | $192,673 |
| Improvements on above | 74,075 |
| Land proved up on 21,720 acres | 63,050 |
| Improvements on above | 22,025 |
| Improvements on unpatented lands, 36,725 acres | 25,795 |
| Improvements on unsurveyed lands | 16,900 |
| 3 quartz-mills | 2,650 |
| Iron pipe and hose | 1,000 |
| 1 shingle-mill | 1,075 |
| 1 flour-mill | 1,400 |
| 5 saw-mills | 3,900 |
| 30 mining ditches | 18,905 |
| Money on hand, notes and other securities | 82,877 |
| 13,200 stock cattle, at $14.77 | 194,901 |
| 21 thoroughbred bulls, at $64.23 | 1,350 |
| 53 thoroughbred cows, at $41.41 | 2,195 |
| 871 milch cows, at $20 | 17,420 |
| 2,410 hogs, at $2.29 | 5,537 |
| Bacon | 400 |
| 9 stallions, at $322.22 | 2,900 |
| 7,863 mixed horses, at $17.86 | 140,254 |
| 2 jacks and jennies | 365 |
| 80 mules, at $24.13 | 1,931 |
| 11 work oxen, at $26.36 | 290 |
| 7,282 sheep, at $1 | 7,282 |
| Farming utensils | 466 |
| Store fixtures | 245 |
| Furniture | 2,333 |
| Goods, wares and merchandise | 48,790 |
| Machinery | 7,168 |
| Musical instruments | 1,925 |
| Vehicles | 12,982 |
| 6 watches, at $50 | 300 |
| 1 wire bridge | 2,000 |
| 1 ferry-boat | 400 |
| Personal property not enumerated | 42,479 |
| Total valuation | $1,000,808 |

Hon. A. F. Parker writes:—

"The western base of Idaho county is washed by the waters of Snake River, and it is bounded on the east by the Bitter Root Divide, forming the State boundary line between Idaho and Montana, a distance of nearly 200 miles from east to west. From north to south it covers a nearly equal distance. Through the center of this vast area courses the Salmon River, draining with its multitudinous tributaries the largest and least known scope of mineral country on the Pacific slope. Through its northern limits flows the Clearwater, draining on the western slope of the Bitter Root Mountains the finest forests of timber on the continent. Its principal agricultural settlement is the great Camas Prairie, an elevated plateau forming a low divide between the Salmon and Clearwater rivers, which at one point are only thirty miles apart. Throughout the region drained by these rivers

are vast areas of unexplored country whose surrounding characteristics indicate an extensive zone containing large deposits of the royal
metals.

" In the heart of the surrounding mountains are the famous placer mines
of Oro Fino, Elk City, Florence, Warrens, and Salmon rivers, names
which, in the early '60s electrified the mining world with their marvelous
output of precious metal, and paved the way for the establishment of the
more enduring industries of cattle-raising and agriculture which now constitute the bulk of its wealth. These old mining camps are still extensively
worked, and are still supplied by means of pack trains which average in
distance traveled ten miles per day. As the distance from the base of supplies is 150 miles, it can be easily seen that only the richest ground can
stand the great expense of this primitive method of transportation.

" The great need of Idaho county is wagon roads and railroads, and,
with the cheaper transportation which these handmaids of civilization
would bring, this scantily settled county would afford sustenance to a very
large mining population, which would work the numerous mining regions
where gold is known to exist in paying quantities. With the development
which railroads bring, ten thousand men would find profitable employment
in mining the golden sands from the rich gravel bars which line the banks
and tributaries of Salmon River from its source to its mouth. The richer
claims on this golden stream are even now worked at a more or less varia-
ble profit, and good prospects are being constantly found. Where wing-
dams have been constructed as high as $2,000 have been taken out in
twenty-four hours. Gold is found in nearly all the tributaries of
the Salmon. They have never yet been carefully prospected for the
wealth they contain, for even the most reckless of enterprising miners
begins to study the situation when freight is from five to fifteen cents per
pound.

"There are hundreds of acres of ground in all the old placer mining camps
which could be profitably worked if the country were made accessible by
wagon roads; and in all the adjacent country on both sides of the Clearwater
and Salmon rivers are great quartz districts, all lying just as nature left
them and awaiting cheaper transportation to be developed into great,
wealthy and productive mining camps. The whole of this great interior in
the heart of Idaho is practically a *terra incognita* of wild and forbidding
aspect, and its development will be necessarily slow, from the fact that it
is isolated and apart from any of the great traveled thoroughfares.

"The placer mining industry still employs a large population, as may
be gathered from the fact that Idaho county leads the list of gold-dust-pro-
ducing counties of the State. Placer mining has hitherto almost exclusively
engaged the attention of its mining population, but within the past few
months important quartz discoveries have been made at several points
within the area of its unprospected mountain ranges. The Bitter Root
Range, forming the eastern boundary of the county and State, is, in reality,
the true backbone of the continent, and it has been less prospected than
any other range, although enough is known of its character and formation

to justify the belief that it is seamed with ribs and veins of gold and silver bearing quartz. The Salmon River Mountains also afford an inviting field for exploration, for the range has scarcely been touched by the pick of the prospector for quartz, and placer mining has been confined to the river bars and the small basins tributary to the main river. The larger forks of the Salmon River are all an unknown country, that cannot but be rich in mineral wealth, from the fact that it is the source from whence the gold of the placer camps was derived. In 'Warren's diggings the quartz interests are already assuming large proportions, and ten-stamp batteries, with furnaces and complete reduction apparatus, as well as several arastras, are kept steadily running on high-grade ore."

This is the largest county in this State, yet in spite of its really wonderful capabilities it has been one of the slowest in development. The lack of transportation facilities is the cause of the comparatively slow growth of Idaho county. Railroads are now in process of construction from the north and northwest, which will doubtless afford the northern portion of this county an outlet for its agricultural products and the State government is now constructing a wagon road which will facilitate the development of the southern portion. Contracts have been let for a good wagon road from Meadows, in Washington county, to Warrens, in Idaho county, and from thence to Mount Idaho, the county seat. The work is under direction of a State commission, of which Hon. N. B. Willey, Lieutenant-Governor, is chairman.

The mines of the western portion of Idaho county have been frequently described and space will not permit a detailed statement of their present condition and prospects. They have been worked for years under the greatest obstacles. Supplies have been carried for 150 miles over difficult trails on the backs of pack animals, and the products of the mines have been returned in the same way. The elevation is considerable, the working season short, and expenses are very heavy. Yet, under all these unfavorable circumstances, the mines have yielded a uniform profit. Could the mines of Warrens district and other mineral districts of Idaho county be reached by railroad and furnished with sufficient capital, it is probable that this section would become one of the greatest producers of precious metals known in the history of mining.

In a recent interview, Lieutenant-Governor N. B. Willey said:

"The wheat crop far surpasses that of any previous year and the prices are satisfactory to the producer. The enormous piles of grain accumulating at shipping points, with a ready market and prompt payment, wreathes the farmer's brow with smiles.

"The mining interests of the north are also in a prosperous condition. In the old placer camp of Elk City numerous discoveries of large veins of auriferous ore give promise of great results as soon as a wagon road can connect that district with the outside world. In Florence the yield of gold, mostly from placer ground, still continues good.

"In Warrens three 5-stamp mills and two arastras are in operation most of the time. The Mayflower mine employs fourteen men, and runs day and night as long as the inclemency of season permits the use of water power. The yield per ton is unknown to any except the owners, but the gross output is quite large.

"The Keystone is worked by an arastra and the ore is reported to yield over $80 per ton, but the vein is quite small, averaging between 6 and 12 inches in thickness. The Giant, owned by G. Reibold, is the largest producer of the camp. For many years the annual output of ore has yielded between $70 and $216 per ton for the entire amount of ore produced. Mr. Reibold has also a complete plant for working silver ore, consisting of roasting furnace, pans, steam supply, retorts and assay office and all necessary equipments. He employs quite a number of men throughout the year. The Wolverine, owned by S. A. Willey, is a very small vein from one to five inches in thickness, but the quantity of precious metal it contains is very unusual. It never pays less than $100 per ton in free gold and the tailings being roasted with salt and worked for silver, produce all the way from 200 to 1,700 ounces per ton of that important metal.

"There are also numerous other properties more or less developed which employ each a few men."

### AGRICULTURE.

The great Camas Prairie is the only portion of Idaho county which is available for agricultural purposes. It is the largest and best body of agricultural land in the State and is rapidly settling up with a desirable and thrifty class of immigrants. This prairie has an altitude of 3,000 feet and is situated on a low divide between the Salmon and Clearwater rivers. The climate is wonderfully bracing and good, the temperature being modified by the warm air rising from the cañons of the great rivers which inclose it, while the warm breath of the never-failing "Chinook" wind causes the open winters, which make it such an unexcelled cattle-raising country. During winter of 1889, which was of exceptional severity, the loss of live stock running on the range without feed did not exceed 2½ per cent. Owing to its isolation and absence of a market—it is 63 miles from Lewiston, the nearest shipping point—the residents of Camas Prairie are almost exclusively dependent upon cattle-raising to consume their products. The society is of a very high standard, and the people are unusually intelligent, hospitable, orderly and thrifty. The county jail has not had an inmate for a long time.

In respect to agriculture, Idaho county contains within her borders an immense amount of fertile land capable of producing any crop that can be raised in the temperate zone without irrigation. The rainfall is always abundant enough to insure heavy crops without irrigation. The varying altitudes of the agricultural lands lend diversity to the products of the county. In the valley lands bordering on the banks of the Salmon and Clearwater rivers, fruits of the choicest kinds are raised and the soil there seems to possess just the right mineral properties for the successful raising of grapes, which are produced so successfully that the richest vineyards of Southern France can not surpass them in quality or quantity. On the higher altitudes of the bench and prairie lands, the cereal crops and the hardier varieties of fruits, such as apples, pears, plums and prunes grow to perfection.

On Camas Prairie the average yield of wheat, taking one year with another, is 30 bushels per acre; oats, 50 bushels; barley, 60 bushels; timothy, two tons per acre. In exceptionally favorable years these yields are more than doubled. The soil is a rich, black loam of unexcelled fertility and productiveness. General O. O. Howard, who conducted the Nez Percé war of 1877, thus describes Camas Prairie:

"The broad and beautiful Camas Prairie opens out before you as you set your back to Craig's Mountain and look towards the southeast. The straight road in your front leads from you to Grangeville and Mount Idaho. What a beautiful stretch of rolling prairie land! Where is there richer soil or finer prospects? Towards the right is the "Snake country." The Salmon, which flows northwesterly, empties into the Snake not more than twenty miles to the southwest. The Cottonwood Creek, heading near by, runs easterly into the curvilinear Clearwater, twenty miles off, and the Rocky Cañon Creek, close by, shoots out southwest to join the Salmon, while White Bird, before described, makes its remarkable cañon and empties into the Salmon a few miles further up that stream. This country is as well watered as Eden, and as fertile as any garden which has been much longer under cultivation. When the Pacific railroads shall be completed the Camas Prairie will not be despised."

There is much land available for agricultural purposes that has not yet been surveyed. The dereliction of Congress in not making sufficient appropriations for the proper survey of the agricultural lands on the public domain greatly retards the settlement and development of the State in general and of Idaho county in particular.

### STOCK·RAISING.

Great as are the resources of Idaho county for agricultural and kindred pursuits they are even greater for pastoral purposes. It is in the future immense herds of cattle and horses that will range over her beautiful plains, mountains, mesas, and meadows, finding everywhere the most abundant, nutritious, and natural pasturage the whole year round, and accumulating at a rate of increase unparalleled elsewhere, that her wealth will roll up in mighty volumes, far eclipsing that ever derived from her mines in the past. Already the stock-raising interest has taken its place as a bulwark of support and source of revenue to the county, and in the future it will easily assume a position of greater prominence, because of the boundless area of pasture land in this county.

### THE BITTER ROOT MOUNTAINS.

The Bitter Root Mountains, or rather the western slope, situated in Idaho county, are the least known part of the State. The whole region from Cœur d'Alene on the north to the Sawtooth range on the south is practically a *terra incognita*. Two Indian trails, the Lolo and Nez Percé, are the sole means of communication with the Montana side. This range is drained by the Clearwater River, the noblest of all the tributaries of the great Snake River. In point of altitude the Bitter Root divide is not lofty; the highest points not exceeding 8,000 feet elevation above sea level. The range is densely timbered and possesses some of the finest forests of cedar on the continent, besides a very fine and durable growth of pine, fir, spruce, and other evergreens. The only residents of this great region are the inhabitants of the old mining camps of Oro Fino on the north, and of Elk City on the southern tributaries of the Clearwater.

Recent explorations in Elk City mining district have led to the discovery of two very large and promising quartz belts. One of these is situated about fifteen miles east of Elk City, and embraces the Red River and Dixie regions. This belt has been traced for a distance twenty-five miles in length, and seems to be on a line with the mineral belt of Warrens and Alton districts in central Idaho heretofore described. In the neighborhood of Elk City this quartz belt is from five to ten miles wide. The date of discovery is so recent, and so difficult and expensive are the means of transportation in the present isolated condition of the country, that but little prospecting has been done to ascertain the real value of the district.

The second belt and the one which promises to eclipse all and anything heretofore discovered in this State is situated at a distance of ten miles south of Elk City. It is on what is known as the Deadwood range of mountains which forms the back-bone between the American and Crooked River water-sheds. These two streams with Red River form the south fork of Clearwater. The mineral zone is wonderfully well defined throughout the Deadwood Range, and exposes more and a better variety and quality of surface quartz than any other camp on the continent. The first prospects were only discovered in the spring of 1889, and of course but little development has been done, owing to the extreme isolation of the country. Nevertheless the showing already made promises, in the fullness of time, to make the greatest and best quartz mining camp on the Pacific coast. The ledges are large and well defined and the ore carries black sulphurets, and oxides and pyrites of iron. Assays of samples taken from the surface of sixteen different claims in this belt show a wonderful uniformity of value throughout, the highest realizing $30 in gold and $6 in silver per ton; the lowest $2 in gold and $4 in silver per ton. The ores are all of the concentrating variety and facilities for their reduction on the cheapest scale exist in the neighborhood. The mines overlook the American River on one side of the divide and Crooked River on the other, and the topographical features of the country are such that the ore can be mined at a very low figure. It is said that no other district in Idaho offers such opportunities for profitable investment in great mining properties as the Elk City region, nor such sure and certain returns, or growth and value of the same, as these new fields of operation open to investors. There are quartz mines in the neighborhood which have been operated successfully for many years by individual enterprise.

The Elk City basin is a large and beautiful park-like valley with wood, water, grass, and game in unlimited abundance. When the country becomes more accessible it will be a great resort for tourists, sportsmen and prospectors. Its elevation is not more than 4,500 feet above tide-water and quartz mining operations can therefore be carried on the year round without interruption.

## KOOTENAI COUNTY.

| | Assessment Values. |
|---|---|
| Improved land patented, 95,000 acres........................ | $ 251,115 50 |
| Improvements on above................................ | 24,275 00 |
| Improvements on unpatented lands, 32,000 acres.......... | 50,855 00 |
| Town lots........................................ | 266,331 00 |
| Improvements on town lots............................ | 59,635 00 |
| Western Union Telegraph Company................... | 13,540 00 |
| Washington and Idaho Railroad Company............. | 359,580 00 |
| Spokane Falls and Idaho Railroad Company........... | 40,500 00 |
| Buildings on same.................................. | 1,700 00 |
| Cœur d'Alene Railway and Navigation Company...... | 10,500 00 |
| Rathdrum Water-works.............................. | 500 00 |
| Cœur d'Alene Water-works......................... | 4,000 00 |
| Chloride and Weber toll road...................... | 500 00 |
| 7 saw-mills ...................................... | 14,500 00 |
| 7 shingle-mills................................... | 3,500 00 |
| Railroad stock assessed by county................. | 85,657 71 |
| Steamer.......................................... | 31,800 00 |
| Store-ships and hulks............................. | 150 00 |
| Lime-kilns........................................ | 800 00 |
| Barges............................................ | 2,800 00 |
| Small boats....................................... | 150 00 |
| Money on hand.................................... | 400 00 |
| Solvent credit.................................... | 5,346 25 |
| Goods, wares and merchandise..................... | 53,650 00 |
| Brandies and other liquors........................ | 2,000 00 |
| Harness, robes and saddles ....................... | 3,500 00 |
| 2,000 cattle, at $12.25............................ | 24,500 00 |
| 160 colts, at $20................................. | 3,200 00 |
| 2 bulls, at $100.................................. | 200 00 |
| 1,240 American cows, at $25 ...................... | 31,000 00 |
| 240 hogs......................................... | 1,200 00 |
| 4 thoroughbred horses, at $300.................... | 1,200 00 |
| 300 half-breed horses, at $50..................... | 15.000 00 |
| 250 American horses............................... | 20,000 00 |
| 450 ponies at $25................................. | 11,250 00 |
| 60 mules, at $58.................................. | 3,480 00 |
| 50 oxen, $50...................................... | 2,500 00 |
| Machinery........................................ | 5,000 00 |
| Store fixtures.................................... | 8,000 00 |
| Furniture ........................................ | 3,000 00 |
| Lumber .......................................... | 42,000 00 |
| Musical instruments.............................. | 3,750 00 |
| Sewing-machines.................................. | 1,800 00 |
| Wagons and Vehicles.............................. | 14,000 00 |
| Watches ......................................... | 2,100 00 |
| Shingles ......................................... | 493 75 |
| Total valuation.................................. | 1,480,959 21 |

Kootenai is the northernmost county of Idaho, forming the extreme end of what is called the "Panhandle." It is nearly 200 miles long and about ninety miles wide. The products consist of vegetables of every description, cereals, and excellent apples and pears. Here are large bodies of fir, tamarack, and pine. Of the latter hundreds of car loads are every year shipped east and west to less favored sections in Montana and Washington.

"A prophet is not without honor save in his own country" will apply equally to a region of wonderful resources as to a person. Good water, rich mines, fine timber, great water-power, temperate climate, and the best of agricultural land are the characteristics of this county; yet few Eastern people are aware that such a favored region exists in the far-away North-west—

Where land is as cheap as the wind that blows,
And gold in every rivulet flows.

Not only is this a remarkable region of silver and gold, but the immense forests of fir, tamarack, and pine will furnish lumber for ages to come. Then there are the beautiful lakes of Pend d'Oreille, Cœur d'Alene, Hayden, Fish, Spirit, and numerous others, all filled with delicious trout, and towering mountains, on which graze countless herds of carriboo, deer, elk, and mountain goat. Brooks of sparkling ice-cold water go on and on to the big Columbia, and finally add their portion to the Pacific Ocean.

The public are generally familiar with the immense output of placer gold from the Cœur d'Alene country in 1884, 1885, 1886, 1887, and 1888, and still later the thousands upon thousands of tons of high grade silver ore from the quartz leads of that district, yet they do not know that in the northern part of Kootenai county there is a placer region which has for over twenty years yielded golden sands in paying quantities. Sullivan Creek, the Kaniskee Lake country, and the whole Pend d'Oreille region may be instanced as placer districts which have yielded thousands in the past, and are still adding their wealth to the prospector's buckskin purse.

Then the great quartz-belt, the like of which the world has never seen, crops out at irregular intervals in Kootenai county, and even extends into British possessions. It appears in the Webber group, Jumbo, Eagle and other properties around Chloride, and the Homestake, in Granite Creek district. Then it disappears beneath the Pend d'Oreille Lake, and finally out again, six miles north of Hope. Next we find it on the Yak, and there it goes on grander, stronger, richer, until it reaches the big silver leads of the Kootenai Mining and Smelting Company.

There is no more healthful region in Idaho. Streams, lakes, and mountains combine to make natural scenery of unrivaled beauty. Sites for homes of the greatest lovliness and comfort are open alike to rich and poor. New settlers are constantly coming in, yet still there is room.

There are as yet few valuable public buildings; but the county is new, and the enterprising settlers are gradually providing schools and other accessories of the best civilization.

The population of Kootenai county is placed by the Federal census of 1890 at 4,107. Its total assessed value for 1889 was $788,599.57: for 1890 it is $1,480,959.21, showing an increase of 86 per cent. In proportion to population the wealth of Kootenai county heads the list in Idaho. Its growth is in railway mileage, agriculture, forest products, and mining.

The county is attracting attention for many reasons. First is the diversity of its resources. Its forests will furnish employment for men and money for the next hundred years. It has a larger variety of timber than other counties of Idaho, and it will become the seat of manufactures on the most extensive scale. Its climate and soil facilitate agricultural productions of the greatest variety and abundance. It is said to be the best watered county for hundreds of miles, as it has large lakes as well as deep and broad rivers. Its mines are constantly increasing in value and productiveness. All these resources are combined by easy water and railway communication, facilitating exchange of products and giving employment to all kinds of labor.

In natural scenery Kootenai can not be excelled. Thousands of tourists find its lakes, rivers, mountains and valleys a perpetual fund of health and pleasure. There is no pleasanter spot in the Union during July and August—no location better deserving the title of "the hunter's paradise." It is on the great northern highways of transcontinental traffic, hence is easily and cheaply accessible, and the supplies necessary for human comfort are readily procurable.

The county government is well managed, towns and villages are growing, and the home-seeker and investor from distant States will find in Kootenai much to form an enduring attraction. Either through local enterprise or through the State emigration bureau facts more precise and in greater detail ought soon to be gathered and published concerning this beautiful and prosperous county.

## LATAH COUNTY.

|  | Assessment Values. |
|---|---|
| Spokane and Palouse Railway Company | $13,950 |
| Oregon Railway and Navigation Company | 22,700 |
| Improved land patented, 234,258 acres | 1,601,145 |
| Improvements on same | 335,082 |
| Money on hand | 140,941 |
| 6,111 stock cattle | 54,999 |
| 50 thoroughbred bulls, at $60 | 3,000 |
| 2,761 milch cows, at $15 | 41,415 |
| 181 cows and bulls, at $30 | 5,430 |
| Store fixtures | 3,126 |
| Furniture | 9,000 |
| Goods, wares, and merchandise | 149,171 |
| Harness, robes and saddles | 8,464 |
| 2,181 hogs | 2,181 |
| 27 thoroughbred stallions and mares, at $500 | 13,500 |
| 34 graded stallions, at $200 | 6,800 |
| 3,220 American horses, at $40 | 128,800 |
| 4,120 Spanish horses, at $12 | 49,440 |
| Jacks and jennies | 1,200 |
| 419,000 feet lumber | 1,381 |
| Saw-logs | 51 |
| 109 mules, at $26 | 2,834 |
| 407 musical instruments | 12,210 |
| 51 oxen, at $20 | 1,020 |
| 903 sewing-machines | 4,515 |
| 319 sheep | 319 |
| 1,191 wagons and vehicles | 17,865 |
| 2,119 cords wood | 2,119 |
| Other personal property | 138,505 |
| Total valuation | $2,771,143 |

The county of Latah has an area of about 1,100 square miles, of which it is fair to estimate that at least three-fourths can be easily cultivated. The lands are high, rolling prairie, covered in their virgin state with a dense growth of bunch grass. The soil is a deep black loam, upon which immense crops of all the cereals and less tender fruits can be raised. The statistics given in the accompanying tables are the most emphatic comment upon the productiveness of the soil, showing, as they do, that already an annual yield of grain and seeds aggregating three and one-third million bushels, has been attained. When all the agricultural lands of this county are brought under cultivation it may fairly be estimated that the production will exceed the present yield of the entire State.

Springs of water are abundant, irrigation is unnecessary, and droughts unknown.

The county contains an abundance of timber for all purposes, consisting of pine, fir, spruce, tamarack, and cedar. The climate is extremely healthy and pure, the mortality rate in all diseases being very light compared with other countries.

There are three flouring mills within the county limits, whose output is about 40,000 barrels per annum. There are eight saw-mills, which produce annually 15,000,000 feet of lumber.

The rapid grawth of this most prosperous county is shown by comparing the assessment returns of 1889 and 1890. The total assessed value of the property of [Latah county in 1889, was $1,203,192; in 1890 it is given as above, $2,771,143. This is an increase of 130.3 per cent in one year, a growth not equaled by any county in this State, and it is possible not equaled by any important county in the United States.

The foundation of the remarkable prosperity of this county is agriculture. There are 234,258 acres of improved lands for which Government patents have been received. The wheat lands have produced 40 bushels to the acre, and other grains have had a proportionate yield. The total yield of wheat, oats, barley and flax-seed is estimated by a careful authority at 2,925,000 bushels. The hay product is reported at 35,000 tons. And this is but a beginning of the prosperity of Latah county, for it is asserted that 400,000 acres of the best agricultural land still await cultivation, besides 192,000 acres of forest land.

Stock-raising is also an important industry in this county; the lumber business is important; there are fair mining prospects, and a good beginning has been made in manufactures.

During the coming winter a quarter of a million dollars will be expended in railroad building in Latah county. The finest brick is made in great quantities, and excellent building stone abounds. The lumber products of the year ending October 1, 1890, is estimated at 22,000,000 feet. The county possesses four flouring mills of 160 barrels' capacity per day.

At least 22 per cent of the population of this county are Scandinavians, a thrifty, intelligent, industrious class.

Moscow is the county seat of Latah county, and is a wealthy little city of 2,600 inhabitants. The county has built a good court house, at cost of $22,000; private enterprise has provided fair grounds at a cost of $12,000;

the Grand Army of the Republic has here the only public hall in Idaho, held in the interests of that patriotic society. The State has here established its University, for which twenty acres of ground have been purchased, and the foundation stones of a noble building have been laid. Congress has endowed it with a land grant of great value, and the resources of the State are pledged to its support. An enlightened public opinion will gather around the University of Idaho, and make this city the educational crown of the State.

The county seat is supplied with excellent newspapers, and an intelligent legal and medical fraternity. There are two banks with ample capital, and about seventy-five persons and firms engaged in various lines of merchandise. An unusual number of citizens have a State reputation based on their intelligent participation in public affairs. The town has still good openings for men of means and ability, and the industrial forces are fully employed and prosperous.

Other towns in Latah County are prosperous, and the extension of the railway system will develop other towns and communities. The excellent climate, the uniform and abundant rainfall, the activity of the people, and the opportunities for the extension of agriculture and other interests, combine to make the future of this part of Idaho exceedingly bright.

## LEMHI COUNTY.

|  | Assessment Values. |
|---|---:|
| Improved land patented, 12,029 acres | $ 47,719 |
| Improvements on above | 94,735 |
| Improvements on unpatented lands | 75,850 |
| Mining claims | 15,540 |
| Money on hand | 74,378 |
| 10,506 stock cattle, at $11 | 115,567 |
| 39 thoroughbred cows, at $50 | 1,950 |
| 600 graded cows, at $20 | 12,000 |
| Farming utensils | 8,118 |
| Saloon fixtures | 810 |
| Furniture | 1,000 |
| Goods, wares and merchandise | 46,405 |
| Harness, robes and saddles | 5,000 |
| 321 hogs at $5 | 1,605 |
| 3 thoroughbred horses, at $500 | 1,500 |
| 700 graded horses, at $40 | 28,000 |
| 3,012 American horses at $22.60 | 78,098 |
| Jewelry and plate | 500 |
| Law library | 2,000 |
| Machinery | 36,850 |
| Musical instruments | 940 |
| Pianos | 1,560 |
| 6,200 sheep | 8,600 |
| 360 wagons and vehicles | 12,275 |
| Total valuation | $671,000 |

The undeveloped resources of Lemhi county are enormous, and for mining enterprises, no better field can be found. A large number of mines have been located and sufficiently prospected to prove their value, but the introduction of capital is required to work both quartz and placer mines more extensively. Among the prominent mines can be mentioned the Kentuck, owned and operated by the Kentuck Mining Company, and the

Grunter, owned and worked by the original owners. These mines are located at Shoup, and each is equipped with a ten-stamp mill. Large bodies of ore are exposed in both mines, and yield in gold from $12 to $25 per ton. About five miles from Shoup, on Pine Creek, is located the property of a Philadelphia company, comprising the Fissure, Humming Bird, and Ready Cash mines, on which a ten-stamp mill has recently been built. The mines promise well and the company is sanguine of success. Still above, on Pine Creek, is another group—the Richmond, Virginia, Pawnee, Lexington, and Uncle Sam. These mines are being opened by the locators, and show large bodies of good ore.

The Dahlonaga mining district comprises all the waters of the North Fork of Salmon River and its tributaries. In this district are located many valuable properties. Among the prominent ones, and concentrated under one management, are the Huron, Oneida, Rose, Sucker, Sucker Extension, Diana, Eureka, Key Stone, and Twin Brothers. These mines have been extensively developed and large quantities of ore exposed.

Near the group above mentioned is the Emeralda mine. This property has been worked by the locator for years, and is developed to a depth of over 400 feet, and in tunnels and drifts nearly 2,000 feet, exposing a large quantity of high-grade ore. On this property is a ten-stamp mill and furnaces for roasting concentrates.

Within this district are other good properties, including the William Edwards, Tiger and Rattler, on which tunnels and drifts have been run for over 1,000 feet, showing an immense amount of ore of good quality. The ore in the Dahlonaga district is nearly all high grade.

The Salmon City district has a number of meritorious mines, among which are the Silver Star, Ranges, Eldorado, Freeman, and California. The Silver Star is located about twelve miles north of Salmon City and shows a wonderful outcrop of ore, at least from 10,000 to 15,000 tons in sight, and assays well in both gold and silver.

The Ranges mine is developed by tunnels and shafts to an extent of over 500 feet, and shows a vein of very free-milling gold ore from one to three feet in width, which will work $25 per ton. The Eldorado contains a large body of ore worth $10 per ton. The Freeman and California are promising properties and show large veins of ore worth from $20 to $30 per ton.

Within the last four years a new district situated about ten miles northwest of Salmon City has been named the Eureka district. Within this district are the Red Bird, Daisy, Selina, Bird, Anna, and Comet mines. Much work has been done on these properties with satisfactory results.

On Sandy Creek, about twenty miles southeast of Salmon City, several mines have been located within the past three years and are being successfully worked. The ore shows great value, and in arastra tests yields as high as $60 per ton. A mill is now being erected on these properties.

In the Leesburgh district are many good locations. Among those which have been extensively worked may be mentioned the Haidee, Shoo Fly, and Pioneer. On these mines large bodies of ore are exposed, with a value of from $10 to $50 per ton.

In the Prairie Basin district are the Watch Tower Monument and True Blue mines. These are gold and silver lodes, and a large quantity of ore is in sight.

The Yellow Jacket mines, comprising the North and South America and extensions, are gold-bearing properties and situated about ten miles from Prairie Basin. A ten-stamp mill is running steadily on the property at a good profit.

The Viola mine, located at Nicholia, has been a great lead and silver producer, and several millions of dollars have been taken therefrom.

In the Texas district are a number of very promising silver mines, from which considerable ore has been shipped, yielding from $75 to $300 per ton.

Placer mining is carried on to a considerable extent in this county, but owing to a scarcity of water the past two years the output has been small compared with former seasons. Placer ground is not only abundant, but it is rich. Water can be brought from the large streams to cover thousands of acres, and the ground, instead of being worked as at present, from two to six weeeks each season, can be worked six months with great profit. On Napius Creek and its tributaries, which are within the Leesburgh district, over $10,000,000 have been taken, and still there is a vast amount of gold remaining, probably much more than has already been extracted, but bed rock flumes starting below all the old workings are required.

The most notable placer mine in the county is on Moose Creek, and owned by David McNutt. It is estimated that this property has produced over $500,000. The owner of this valuable mine estimates he has several million dollars remaining in the gravel to be taken out. The flume through which this gravel is washed is seven feet wide by six and one-half feet deep.

The agricultural resources of Lemhi county undeveloped are very large. At present about 15,000 acres are under cultivation, or have been cultivated, and the amount of tillable land in the county aggregates over 400,000 acres, which, with proper facilities for irrigation can nearly all be cultivated. As the average yield of crop is large it can readily be seen what an immense population Lemhi county is capable of supporting.

The lumbering resources are also large. A careful estimate by people well acquainted with all sections of the county places the standing white pine, spruce, and fir timber adapted for lumbering purposes at over 1,000,000,000 feet.

From 40,000 to 50,000 forest trees have been planted, including maple, ash, walnut, chestnut, and other varieties, from 5,000 to 7,000 apple trees, and about 2,000 pear, plum, and cherry trees.

Although the planting of fruit tees did not commence until a comparatively late date, it is thoroughly demonstrated that fruit raising will be a success, as several orchards are now in full bearing.

Skilled mechanics receive $5 per day; miners and millers, $3.50; woodchoppers, $2.50; herders and skilled farm hands, $35 to $45 per month; teamsters, $50 to $60; lumbermen, $40 to $50; cooks, $30 to $40.

Governor Shoup in his report for 1890 gives the following account of Lemhi county:

During the summer of 1866 a party of prospectors discovered rich placer diggings about 17 miles west of the present town of Salmon City, at a place called Leesburgh or Salmon River Basin, and an influx of miners was the result. The basin was in Idaho County, the county seat of which was at Florence, 800 miles distant by the nearest traveled route. Lemhi county was admitted by act of the Territorial Legislature in 1869.

### MINING.

There are a large number of mining districts in the county. Placer mining is still being carried on in Leesburgh Basin, on Moose Creek, and some other localities. Placer ground is very abundant. In many cases it is located in river bars and hills far from streams. Following is a brief notice of some of the most prominent lodes.

The Kaintuck mine is located in Mineral Hill district about 45 miles northwest of Salmon City. Connected with this mine is a fine 10-stamp mill, which has been running almost continuously for five years, producing very satisfactory results. The company has sufficient ore developed to operate the mill for many years.

Near the Kaintuck is a vein known as the Grunter, containing the same quantity and grade of ore. It has a 10-stamp mill and has paid well for years. On the North Fork of Salmon River, in Dahlonega district, are located the Huron, Oneida, Rose, Keystone, Sucker, Golden Circle, Twin Brothers, Bill Edwards, McCarty, Monster, Mammoth, Montgomery, St. Joe, and Sucker Extension lodes. Two mills and several arastras are employed on the ores of this district. The bullion produced is nearly pure gold. On Pine Creek are two mines owned by a Philadelphia company, comprising the Fissure, Ready Cash, and Humming Bird mines. The company has a 10-stamp mill, with which their ore is crushed. On the same creek are the Richmond, Virginia, Pawnee, Lexington, and Uncle Sam. All of these show large bodies of good gold ore. Hon. E. S. Suydam owns a group of mines in this district carrying very high grade gold ore. He has a mill operating near the mines and giving satisfactory results.

There are excellent mines in the Yellow Jacket district. In connection with these mines is a 10-stamp mill. Only gold ores are worked in the mill. There are hundreds of mines in the Spring Mountain, Texas, Pahsamari, and Salmon City districts. A lode was recently discovered in the last named district near the city. Its ore assays in gold, silver, and copper, $450 per ton. The name of the mine is the Orpha.

At Nicolia, in the Lemhi district, is located the Viola group of mines. From 1883 to 1889 it produced largely in lead and silver, 75 per cent of the former and 12 to 40 ounces of silver to the ton. During the year last named the main body of ore became so reduced that the smelter closed down. Development is being pushed and the company will soon have sufficient ore developed to fire up the smelter.

On Sandy Creek, in Sandy Creek District, there is a mill working gold ores from the mines in that district and producing from $30 to $50 per ton.

Salmon City is the county seat of Lemhi county. It is pleasantly located at the confluence of the Salmon and Lemhi rivers, and was laid out in 1867. It is surrounded by a rich agricultural country. It is the supply point for the mines of Leesburgh Basin, Gibbonsville, Shoup, North Fork, and all other points down the river. The supplies for Leesburgh and several other mining camps are transported upon pack animals, but the camps down the river are supplied by means of flat-boats. These are constructed at Salmon City. They never return, but the nails used in their construction are drawn, and the lumber used for building, mining, or other useful purposes. In this way the miners have been supplied with the necessaries of life and the material requisite to pursue their business, for many years. From its location and natural advantages the town is destined to become an important point when the country shall have been connected with the outside world by means of railroads, which does not seem to be far in the future.

Junction is 50 miles from the county seat on the stage road between Salmon City and Nicolia. It is located near the Lemhi River and surrounded by a rich agricultural and stock-raising country. It has a good hotel, hardware, grocery, and drug store, together with other appurtenances of a village.

Gibbonsville is on the North Fork of Salmon River, about 40 miles north of Salmon City. It is surrounded with mines, some of which have been worked profitably for years. Two quartz mills are located near the town.

### AGRICULTURE.

As an agricultural region the valleys of the Lemhi, Salmon River, and Pahsamari cannot be surpassed. Wheat, oats, barley, and all kinds of vegetables return as large a yield to the acre as in the great Snake River Valley. There is a good flour mill near Salmon City, where wheat finds a ready market at $1 per bushel. A home market is found in the mines for oats, barley, and vegetables. Hay is cultivated on a large area, and is fed during the winter to the large herds of cattle and horses in the valleys. Butter making has been one of the most successful and profitable industries for many years. There are many excellent cattle, horse, and sheep ranges in the county.

### TIMBER.

This county is abundantly supplied with timber. It is convenient to all points, but more especially so west of the Salmon River. Much of it is of great size. Neither this nor several succeeding generations are likely to suffer from a scarcity of wood for any of the many purposes to which it is applied.

## LOGAN COUNTY.

|  | Assessment Values. |
|---|---|
| Improved land patented, 44,337 acres | $ 107,785 |
| Improvements on above | 74,300 |
| Improvements on unpatented land, 41,977 acres | 40,737 |
| Western Union Telegraph Company | 10,956 |
| 5 quartz mills | 30,700 |

Assessment Values.

| | |
|---|---:|
| 2 concentrators | 3,500 |
| 1 sampler | 2,000 |
| 2 mining ditches | 1,000 |
| 4 irrigating ditches | 1,500 |
| Oregon Short Line Railway Company | 1,118,325 |
| Money on hand | 5,875 |
| 7,187 stock cattle | 100,534 |
| Farming utensils | 13,805 |
| Fire-arms | 75 |
| Store fixtures | 1,500 |
| Furniture | 2,200 |
| Goods, wares and merchandise | 50,780 |
| Harness, robes and saddles | 8,831 |
| 286 hogs | 1,157 |
| 3,585 cayouse horses | 104,207 |
| Jewelry and plate | 185 |
| Machinery | 21,945 |
| 19 mules | 855 |
| Pianos | 2,000 |
| Railroad rolling stock | 50,000 |
| Sewing machines | 1,930 |
| 13,568 common sheep | 27,134 |
| 406 wagons and vehicles | 7,112 |

Total valuation .................................................................. $1,709,928

Logan county embraces an area of 7,000 square miles, being larger than the States of Connecticut and Rhode Island combined. Shoshone is the present county seat.

Mountain and valley and plain interspersed make up the surface of the county. On the south, running the entire length of the county is the great Snake River Basin. In the northwest is Camas Prairie, a rich agricultural region of 1,400 square miles of tillable land. The great Wood River Valley contains nearly as much more, and there are several smaller valleys branching out from Wood River. The Valleys are surrounded with low-lying foot hills and high mountains whose sides provide excellent grazing, and in whose strongholds are imprisoned ores and minerals of all kinds.

With the single exception of the lava beds on the south, the soil of the county is most productive, yielding rich treasures to the farmer. Camas Prairie is well adapted to wheat growing, and in time may be the granary of Idaho. In the Wood River and other valleys the rich sandy loam can not be excelled. It not only yields large returns in cereals and hardy vegetables, but fruits of all kinds produce abundantly. The mountains are covered to their peaks with the noted bunch-grass, showing a splendid soil. Nearly the entire area of the county is susceptible of profitable cultivation.

The report of the county assessor shows 86,314 acres of improved land, but there are still remaining immense tracts desirable for entry. The great bulk of this lies in the southern part of the county, and can only be redeemed by the mammoth irrigating canals leading from Snake River. the cost of these contemplated canals is too great for private corporations to undertake; but now that the attention of the National Government has been directed to the matter, it is felt that it will only be a matter of a few years until all the land along the Snake River is redeemed. As it is, the land affords an extensive winter range for thousands of head of stock. Logan county is well adapted to the industry of stock-raising. In the winter the mountains and valleys in the northern part of the county are covered to the depth of from three to four feet with snow. This melting in the spring months gives abundance of moisture to maintain a luxurious growth of grass for grazing herds during the summer months. On the approach of winter the herds find a fine winter range along the Snake River, where rain falls during the months that the snow falls in the northern part of the county. By moving stock backwards and forwards from one part of the county to the other on the approach of the change of seasons, stock-men feed their stock from one end of the year to the other without cutting hay. Cattle, horses, and sheep are the varieties raised. Home consumption affords market for a large proportion of the fat cattle and sheep.

*Camas Prairie.*—This is the most important tract of agricultural land in Logan County. It extends east and west on either side of the Malad River, a distance of 100 miles. The tillable area is eighty miles long, and has an average width of about eighteen miles. Every foot of this tract is worth taking up. Over 800 homesteads and pre-emptions have already been filed. Sixty pre-emptions have been filed since July 1, 1889, and but a few years will elapse until the last acre is taken up by home seekers. The prairie is a high plateau at an estimated average altitude of 5,300 feet. Unlike many other portions of Idaho, irrigation is unnecessary. Underneath the rich soil, at a depth of but a foot or two, is a stratum impervious to the water. So the water that soaks into the soil from the melting snow in the mountains remains close to the surface, affording what is called "sub-irrigation." The climate on the prairie is delightful. Snow falls about the middle of December, remaining on the ground till about the middle of March. The weather is not cold; the air being high and dry, the cold is felt but little. As soon as the snow goes off the rancher can begin his plowing. The principal crops are wheat, oats, barley, and hay. The average yield of wheat is thirty-five bushels, oats sixty, and barley fifty. Hon. Ira S. Waring, one of the most extensive farmers on the prairie, raised 8,000 bushels of grain on 125 acres. Ready market for the grain is found close at hand in the mining camps along Wood River. A roller mill at Bellevue has been unable to buy enough wheat to supply its demand. Fruit trees have been set out on all parts of the prairie. All are yet too young to bear, but their thrifty condition promises rich fruitage when they have the age. Hon. W. Y. Perkins, living at Soldier, has a large orchard of plum, apple, and cherry trees. Out of seventy trees set out, but two have died. The prairie is a community of homes. Three towns, Soldier, Crichton, and Corral, have daily mails. Seven school-houses afford educational privileges to all.

The mineral resources of Logan county may properly be embraced in two grand mineral belts, entirely different in their character and product. The older or more developed of these two may be described as producing strictly argentiferous galena of high grade. This district is known as the Mineral Hill mining district, and is located on either side of Wood River, in the immediate vicinity of Bellevue and Broadford. The second district, familiarly known as the Gold Belt, produces gold ores exclusively. Doniphan is the center of this second great mineral belt.

MINERAL HILL MINING DISTRICT.—This lead-silver-bearing belt or zone embraces an area that may properly be defined in boundary as being a parallelogram two miles wide, extending north and south on either side of Wood River, a distance of twelve miles in Logan county, and continuing from the northern boundary of the county in its northerly course a distance of forty or fifty miles in Alturas county. The center of this rich mineral region is located in Galena Gulch, near the town of Broadford, on Wood River, where several of the principal mines are situated. The most prominent of these is the Minnie Moore mine, which has at present the largest development of any mine in the county, or in all the Wood River country. It has reached the depth of 1,100 feet from which the lowest level is projected.

The output of this mine during the last six years has been an average of 3,000 tons of ore per month. The amount of ore produced by this mine during the first seven years has been about 252,000 tons, which has been concentrated to 50,000 tons, of which 65 per cent has been lead and 4,000,000 ounces have been silver. The market value of the lead has been in the neighborhood of four cents per pound, making an aggregate value of the base metal produced by the mine $2,600,000. At the same time the 4,000,000 ounces of silver produced roughly approximated $4,000,000, making a total product of $6,600,000 for the seven years the mine has been in operation. It is safe to say that 25 per cent of this sum has been net profit to the owners. The property is owned in London and is operated by Thomas Carmichael, Esq., through his efficient superintendent, J. M. Kinnear. The plant is unostentatious, but compact, and excellently adapted to the operation of a large mine on a thorough and economical basis.

The second mine in importance in this district is the Queen of the Hills, half a mile distant from the Minnie Moore. It produces a grade and character of ore similar to that of the Minnie Moore. It has been worked incessantly for the last eight years by the owners, a Salt Lake City corporation. It has attained a depth of over 800 feet, and has recently completed a three-compartment shaft. The gross output of the Queen of the Hills has been $1,800,000, and the vein is as well defined as ever. The mine is under the superintendency of Fulton G. Haight.

Along this belt within the limits of Logan county may be mentioned other mines of great promise, the developments of which have not been on so large a scale as those of the Minnie Moore and Queen; but they have made valuable shipments of ore without concentration, and now possess large bodies of ore. By means of milling facilities these will be made mines of great product. Among these are the Michigan Star, Relief, Penobscot, Overland, Pacific Tunnel, Monday, Deadshot and Queen Victoria.

A complete description of the mines of the gold-belt district, in the northwest portion of Logan county, would extend this pamphlet too far, and an abridged description does not do it justice. The mineral product is almost exclusively gold, of which about a quarter million dollars has been so far extracted.  A large expenditure of capital has been made; the properties are no longer prospects, but mines; and a profitable return to the courageous men who have risked so much in their development is no longer a matter of question.

Governor Shoup, says:

"Nothing will permanently hinder the growth of this county.  It is centrally located, has immense bodies of the finest agricultural lands so situated that they can be irrigated at a moderate expense, and the ranchmen have a home market which absorbs far more than they can produce.

" Prices for all kinds of farm products are high, and are likely to remain so for an indefinite period.  They are hampered somewhat by lack of transportation facilities.  A railway across the northern part of Logan county is imperatively needed, and the local business alone would make it profitable.  Some surveys have been made for an east and west line, directly connecting Bellevue and Boisé, and I am hopeful that such a railway will be constructed.

"A revival of the stock industry is also probable.  Prices of live stock are very low and better prices are anticipated.  If stock-raising can be made profitable anywhere it certainly must be remunerative on the immense grazing grounds of Logan County.

"The mining interests have been depressed on account of temporary causes now happily disappearing.  A general revival of mining interest is anticipated in the spring of 1891.  This county has been too long a profitable field for mining development to permit the slightest doubt of its mineral wealth now.  Millions have been mined, and millions more will be extracted from the gold and silver ledges of Logan County.  There are about 300,000 acres of excellent forest land in this county sufficient for fuel and lumber during the next generation.  About 4,000,000 feet of lumber have been manufactured during the past season.

"The county's financial affairs have been well managed, and without burdening the people the commissioners hope soon to be able to erect permanent county buildings.

" Bellevue is the largest town of this county; has an excellent flouring mill, a valuable system of water works, a fine public school building, and stores and residences which show the wealth and taste of its enterprising inhabitants.  By a vote of a considerable majority of the people, the county seat has been relocated at this point, but the people of Shoshone have asked a hearing in the matter before the courts.

"Shoshone is the junction of the Oregon Short Line and its Wood River branch, and is gaining considerable trade from the constantly growing agricultural and grazing regions which surround it.  Shoshone has also, a fine graded school and a substantial school building, excellent churches, permanent stores and warehouses, and extensive car repair shops used by the railway company.  The Camas Prairie towns have not grown largely during the past year, but are permanently established as business centers.

"Attention is called to the valuable water-power furnished by the rapid flowing Wood River. A line of profitable manufacturing establishments ought to be located in the towns and villages bordering this stream, and make the broad Wood River Valley as famed for manufacturing as for mining, agriculture and stock raising."

## NEZ PERCES COUNTY.

|  | Assessment Values. |
|---|---:|
| Improved land patented, 100,564 acres | $ 623,399 |
| Improvements on above | 76,777 |
| Improvements on unpatented lands | 5,872 |
| Spokane and Palouse Railway Company | 36,790 |
| Municipal bonds | 5,960 |
| Money on hand | 26,865 |
| 837 calves | 6,536 |
| 342 beef cattle | 3,834 |
| 4,014 stock cattle | 52,872 |
| 664 colts | 8,110 |
| 98 thoroughbred cows | 2,513 |
| 458 American cows | 7,745 |
| 530 graded cows | 10,781 |
| Farming utensils | 3,381 |
| Fire-arms | 879 |
| Saloon fixtures | 1,795 |
| Furniture | 9,520 |
| Goods, wares and merchandise | 80,295 |
| Harness, robes and saddles | 5,112 |
| 1,700 hogs | 3,440 |
| 48 thoroughbred horses | 4,505 |
| 1,924 graded horses | 33,281 |
| 1,258 American horses | 37,354 |
| Jacks and jennies | 125 |
| Miscellaneous library | 250 |
| Lumber | 680 |
| Machinery | 12,485 |
| 75 mules | 1,785 |
| Musical instruments | 798 |
| Pianos | 3,535 |
| Sewing machines | 1,959 |
| 17,196 sheep | 25,182 |
| Wagons and vehicles | 11,147 |
| 90 watches | 1,107 |
| Wood | 1,570 |
| Property not enumerated | 7,078 |
| Ferries | 1,250 |
| Total valuation | $1,079,850 |

The Census Bureau returns the population of this county at 2,594. This little handful of people must be remarkably industrious and prosperous to own property worth $2,500,000, raise 938,000 bushels of grain, 40,000 bushels of vegetables, and 3,300 tons of hay, besides participating in all the other activities of trading, stock growing and manufacturing people. The estimate of 5,200 inhabitants, given in report of 1889, is much nearer the facts. The most cautious investigator of this question has never placed the population of this county below 4,000, and indeed it is hardly conceivable that this small number could transact the business of Nez Perces.

The number of acres of land under cultivation in this county has increased 11 per cent in the last twelve months. In the same time final proof has been made on 5,190 acres of farm land and 3,580 acres of Government land has been entered. All branches of agriculture and stock-raising continue steadily prosperous. The county has few of the features of a frontier settlement, but has a peculiar thrift, steadiness, and permanence more generally characteristic of Eastern communities.

Nez Perces county receives the united flow of the largest rivers of Idaho. It is considered the best watered portion of the Northwest. The climate is mild and uniform. Its production of fruit increases year by year and its quality and variety are not excelled on the continent. The best nurseries exist in this county, and their ample supply of young trees and vines is sold over four growing States. The last two years have demonstrated the fact that grapes of all varieties can be successfully grown on the dry hills and ridges facing the Clear Water and Snake rivers, without irrigation, and there are several thousand acres of this land that will receive attention in the near future.

The fish industry is also destined soon to receive marked attention, as the rivers abound with salmon, and the near approach of the railroad will soon furnish a market and also furnish cheaper and more rapid transportation for all other products.

The forest lands of this county are estimated at 200,000 acres, and an ample supply of lumber of the best quality is thus assured for many years. There are also about 150,000 acres of agricultural lands, and 225,000 acres of grazing land still undeveloped and unused. In fact a population of 15,000 persons can easily find room and comfortable homes in Nez Perces County. Schools and churches abound. The pioneers of this county believe in education. The first academy instituted in Idaho was located at Lewiston, the beautiful capital of Nez Perces county, and the same city was the first or nearly the first to organize a system of graded schools with modern methods and appliances.

The city of Lewiston is one of the finest trading points in Idaho. Population 849. It is the gate-way to the supplies required by the immense county of Idaho, and through which the products of that great county pour. The southern portion of Shoshone county has long procured its supplies at Lewiston. Its well capitalized banks, immense grain depots, and great wholesale merchandise houses draw business from a broad area of rapidly developing country. The title to the larger portion of the Indian reservation will soon be extinguished, and Nez Perces will then come to the front as one of the most inviting fields for emigration known to the Northwest. The county is well provided with public buildings and its public affairs are well administered with wise economy and enterprise. Lewiston has a board of trade, which may be addressed for further information.

Nez Perces has also mining resources as yet undeveloped, but attracting more and more attention from practical miners.

## ONEIDA COUNTY.

| | Assessment Values. |
|---|---:|
| Improved land patented, 53,132 acres. | $ 212,531 |
| Improvements on the same | 114,929 |
| Improvements on unpatented land | 48,902 |
| Telegraph lines | 3,883 |
| Irrigating ditches | 21,560 |
| Oregon Short Line Railway Company | 139,380 |
| Utah and Northern Railway Company | 107,250 |
| 11,297 stock cattle, at $12 | 135,562 |
| 1,525 colts, at $15 | 22,875 |
| 37 graded cows, at $16 | 59,200 |
| Farming utensils | 2,695 |
| Store fixtures | 890 |
| Furniture | 8,050 |
| Goods, wares and merchandise | 25,530 |
| Wheat | 500 |
| Oats | 450 |
| Harness, saddles and robes | 1,625 |
| 3,605 graded horses | 116,063 |
| Machinery | 18,510 |
| Musical instruments | 1,575 |
| Sewing machines | 5,025 |
| 18,000 graded sheep. | 16,225 |
| Solvent credits | 10,500 |
| Vehicles | 13,300 |
| Total valuation | $1,086,990 |

The county of Oneida is more closely settled, with possibly one or two exceptions, than any other portion of Idaho. It is strictly an agricultural and stock raising county. It has no mountain ranges of towering height, but its hills are of sufficient elevation to receive every winter a heavy fall of snow and provide an adequate water supply.

This county is a noble illustration of what quiet industry, economy, and old-fashioned thrift will do. The larger portion of the country is aside from the great lines of commerce; its railroad facilities are limited indeed; it has no great manufactures or mines; there is but slight rain fall; yet in face of all discouragements more than 100,000 acres of land have been reclaimed by irrigation; small and well-tilled farms have yielded a bountiful return; improved grades of live-stock flourish on its meadows, and year by year the number of free-holding families increases and the tax-roll grows.

A very large proportion of both the earlier and later settlers are Welsh. There is no need to erect jails or poor-houses for such men. All they need is a government which will protect them from disturbances; they themselves are orderly and honest. Many in early times were infatuated with Mormonism and Mormon practices, but their sturdy independence and good sense are prompting many withdrawals from that misguided society.

Reference to the statistics given in the various tables accompanying this work shows the rank of this county in the production of grain and live-stock. Its growth from year to year is equaled by few other localities. There are four flouring mills, all good mills, and the one at Franklin probably the costliest in the State. The North Star Woolen Mill, also at Franklin, has in the past produced excellent yarns. The population of Franklin is growing. The place is exceptionally prosperous, and is an aggregation of homes and comfort. Preston, Weston, and Samaria are handsome agricultural villages. Malad is the county seat. It contains a population of about 1,200 and has about thirty business houses. The court house and furnishing cost $20,000; the jail $5,000.

There are still about 6,000 acres of forest land. There are eight saw-mills, whose united production last year was 2,500,000 feet of lumber.

The grazing lands of the county embrace about 500,000 acres. The present area of farming land probably can not be very largely increased without the construction of a comprehensive system of storage reservoirs for water.

## OWYHEE COUNTY.

| | Assessment values. |
|---|---:|
| Improved land patented, 15,028 acres | $ 54,222 |
| Improvements on above | 42,860 |
| Improvements on unpatented lands, 40,600 acres | 82,650 |
| 250 mining claims, improvements | 13,250 |
| 6 quartz mills | 15,000 |
| 2 concentrators | 20,000 |
| 6 mining ditches | 1,850 |
| 210 irrigating ditches | 15,000 |
| Silver City Telegraph Company | 810 |
| Silver City Telephone Company | 990 |
| Money on hand | 3,025 |
| 2,200 calves | 15,400 |
| 13,875 stock cattle, at $11 | 152,325 |
| Farming utensils | 11,800 |
| Saloon fixtures | 7,167 |
| Goods, wares, and merchandise | 32,000 |
| Harness, robes, and saddles | 7,940 |
| 590 hogs, at $4 | 2,360 |
| 8,807 American horses | 203,481 |
| 75 jacks and jennies | 1,500 |
| Machinery | 30,000 |
| 50 mules, at $40 | 2,000 |
| Musical instruments | 1,200 |
| 17 pianos | 1,870 |
| 58,660 sheep, at $1.60 | 93,856 |
| Vehicles and wagons | 1,800 |
| Furniture | 9,760 |
| Total valuation | 824,116 |

This county lies in the southwest corner of Idaho, and is noted no less for its grazing lands than for its wealth in mines and mining industries. The Owyhee mines, as they are called, were discovered as long ago as 1863, about nine miles in a westerly direction from Silver City, on what is known as Jordan Creek, said creek having been named after the discoverer of the placer mines thereon. In a short time the prospecting party, of which Jordan was a member, discovered War Eagle Mountain and several quartz lodes which have since produced a great amount of money, and are being worked at the present time. The lodes so far discovered lie within an area of about twenty miles square. They vary in width from two to sixty feet, while the ores assay from a trace of gold or silver into thousands of dollars.

This has been one of the greatest gold and silver producing counties in the State, having turned into the coffers of the world something like $26,000,000 between the time of the discovery of its mines up to 1876, when, upon the collapse of the Bank of California, capital was withdrawn from the mines, and the life of the camp was left to be sustained by individuals residing therein. Though capital had been withdrawn the mines still continued to yield, which fact finally attracted the attention of outsiders, who came in and invested considerable money in the mines, and are now working the same. Some of the most prominent of the mines now being worked are hereinafter described as follows, to wit:—

*The Oro Fino Group.*—This group of eight mines belongs to the Oro Fino Mining Company, limited, of London, England, and are being worked under the immediate supervision of Mr. Dalby Morkill, the managing director. The group is called after the Oro Fino, a mine which has produced in the past $1,800,000 and is destined soon to produce as much more. The lode is situated on War Eagle Mountain, three miles distant from Silver City. The vein is a true fissure varying from two to six feet in width, carrying free milling ore of gold and silver. The shaft has reached the depth of 307 feet while the mine has not been stoped out to that depth. Levels already started on the mine before it was purchased by the company now owning it have been continued with good results. A lode of very rich ore has been discovered for a distance of 120 feet in length, reaching upward about 100 feet, or as far as developed. At a recent test, ore from this lode milled $225 per ton, the product being nearly all gold. Over the mine is a most substantial shaft-house with hoisting machinery capable of working the mine to a depth of 1,500 feet, while at Silver City is the new Oro Fino twenty-stamp steam quartz mill. The Oro Fino group of mines is covered by ten locations, patents for which have been applied for.

*Poorman Group.*—This group of mines covers an area of about one-half a mile in width by one mile in length, and is composed of eight or ten lodes, the principal of which being the celebrated Poorman, the Belle Peck, Oso, Illinois Central, South Poorman, Silver Cord, and Jackson. All these mines have produced more or less, while the Poorman has yielded millions. United States patents have been applied for, for this group of mines. The property was purchased about one year since by a syndicate of gentlemen then living in London, among whom was Mr. J. C. Kemp van Ee, who is now residing at Silver City, and managing the property. Although he has had charge of the same but a short time it has yielded handsomely, and is now being developed under his direction by cross-cuts, tunnels, and drifts. He has opened up a rich body of ore in the Oso, which shows free gold in considerable quantity. In the Illinois Central he has opened up about 500 feet in the length of pay ore by sixty feet in depth. How much deeper the chute extends can only be determined by the drill and pick. The Poorman mine will be tapped by a tunnel run from the Belle Peck mine at a depth of about 700 feet, and this once celebrated lode will then be worked through the Belle Peck tunnel.

*Stormy Hill.*—This property is situated southeast of the Poorman lode, and belongs to Mr. A. J. Sands, Owyhee county. The lode averages about three feet in width, and has a shaft on it ninety feet deep. Levels have been run each way from the bottom of the shaft in good ore. The ore is free milling and is easily extracted from the mine.

*Empire.*—This lode is among the best developed mines in the camp, having a shaft sunk on it to the depth of about 700 feet, with a man-way from top to bottom. Drifts are run on the vein every hundred feet from the surface to the bottom of the shaft, making in all seven levels, while from the bottom of the shaft a drift has been run north for about 700 feet. There is a great amount of ore in this vein that will pay handsomely over all expenses of extracting and reduction. A good ore house and hoisting works stand over the mine, the machinery being in perfect working order. The property belongs to Hon. J. I. Crutcher and Mr. J. L. Crutcher.

*Mahogany* is the property of Mr. T. Regan. Has been developed to a depth of 800 feet by shaft, and drifts run on the load   Vein averages about two feet in width, and has produced $400,000.

*Morning Star* is situated about one quarter of a mile north of Silver City, and is owned by Messrs. Stoddard, Townsend, and Smith. Lode averages two feet in width, and has shaft sunk to a depth of 225 feet. Mine has produced about $750,000.

*Black Jack.*—This property is owned by W. H. Deevey, of Silver City. Lode, 1,500 feet in length by 100 feet in width. Has been worked to a depth of about 200 feet by shaft and tunnel. Stopes have been run and ore extracted which has yielded over $300,000. The vein will average four feet in width, incased in porphyry. The ore is free milling, carrying gold and silver. The property is a valuable one, and can be worked to a great advantage by tunnel from Blue Gulch, which would cut the mine nearly 1,000 feet deep. This lode is situated on Florida Mountain.

*Seventy-nine,* owned by W. B. Knott, is situated northwest of the Black Jack. Has been developed by cross-cut and drifts, showing a vein that will average six feet wide of ore that will run from $20 to $50 per ton. There are thousands of tons of ore in sight, which only need extracting and reduction to place the owner beyond all financial wants.

*Phillips & Sullivan* is owned by Isaac Phillips and J. F. Sullivan, of Silver City. The lode location is 1,500 feet in length by 600 feet in width. The vein averages three feet in width. Has been worked for about one year by shaft and drifts, and has produced $40,000 in gold bullion.

*Wagontown District.*—The mines in this district were discovered in 1876 by J. W. Stoddard, who, in company with others, located the Stoddard lode, the first mine recorded in that district.

The lode is located in a northerly and southerly direction; is 1,500 feet in length by 600 feet in width. Has been opened by tunnel, showing lode eight feet wide; ore free milling, yielding on an average $60 per ton. It is the property of Messrs. T. Regan and C. M. Hays, and is now being prospected by Hon. J. P. Jones and Mr. T. Regan.

*Wilson.*—This is probably the largest and richest mine in Idaho. It lies northwest of the Stoddard, is in the same formation, and is worked by a cross-cut run to cut the lodes, and then by drifts. The property is owned by Christian and Louis Wahl, of Chicago, and Capt. J. R. De Lamar, of De Lamar, Owyhee county. There are three veins in this location, though from the formation some would call them all one, or a mountain of quartz mineralized. The first is called Voshay, being a lode about fifteen feet in width; the second, the Wilson, thirty feet in width; and the third the Seventy-seven, it being seventy-seven feet in width. The veins have all been run on and opened up in good shape, showing, it is estimated, over 300,000 tons of ore that will mill from $15 to $200 per ton. The ore is easily extracted, two men being able to keep a twenty-five stamp mill running. Indeed only about one-half the ore extracted is crushed, the remainder being simply screened and thrown into the pans. The bullion produced is high grade in gold. A portion of one of the lodes named produces silver ore that runs over $500 per ton per car load. This character of ore is being shipped almost daily to the railroad, distant from the mine about forty-eight miles, where it is loaded on the cars and shipped to Denver for reduction. Captain De Lamar has erected a ten-stamp mill on Jordan Creek, about half a mile distant from the mine, which will soon start up on the gold ore from the mine. He is also constructing a tramway with which to run the ore from the lode to the mill.

The latest information from the mines at De Lamar is of the most encouraging character. Development work has gone on systematically and at great cost, and the ore now in sight has been estimated worth $6,000,000. Mills with improvements of the best and latest invention have been erected. It is said that $2,000,000 have been offered for the De Lamar mining system and declined. The greatest need of the place now is railway communication, to take ore out and bring in timber and mining supplies.

This locality, which two years ago boasted but a trifling number of wretched cabins, now has a hotel which would be a credit to a substantial town, a school-house, stores and numerous comfortable dwellings. No one would be surprised to see 2,500 people at De Lamar within one year. The present output of the De Lamar mines is said to average $60,000 per month, or $700,000 per year. A correspondent says:

"De Lamar spent three years in opening this property, and while building his extensive surface improvements, which includes a modern 80-ton pan amalgamating mill, for the last twelve months since production began, he has with this comparatively small plant taken out $750,000 in gold and silver, and claims that when the north and south railroad is assured, so that he can supply himself with all necessaries for a larger plant (including vast quantities of mining timber and fuel), he will at once begin the erection of works that will reduce 500 tons of ore each twenty-four hours, which at $20 per ton value saved will give him a daily production of $10,000 per day, or $300,000 monthly, or $3,600,000 per annum— equal to the grandest mines in mining history."

Sommercamp Group of Mines.—This group of mines lies west of the Wilson, and is owned by Mr. W. F. Sommercamp, Sr., of Silver City. Unlike many other mine owners in this and other districts, Mr. Sommercamp has worked his mines with the view of opening them up and showing the value of his property. He has been about six years in running cross-cuts and drifts on lodes found, and as a result can show thousands of tons of fair milling ore, some of which will assay into the thousands of dollars. The lodes in this group are all large and well defined.

In speaking of Owyhee county Governor Shoup remarks:

"The increasing mineral wealth of this county is likely to obscure its agricultural standing. Its growth in this regard is shown by the fact that in 1889 but 4,685 acres had been patented, while in 1890 15,028 acres are reported. There are about 18,000 head of stock cattle in this county, about 15,000 range horses, and 75,000 sheep. The grazing lands are almost limitless in extent and the melting snows of the Owyhee range nourish a prolific growth of native grass. The irrigating system has been extended under the direction of intelligent capitalists, and it is probable that the area of cultivated lands will be increased 100 per cent during the next year. The ranches are large and well managed. But a small portion of the waters of Owyhee county have yet been utilized for purposes of irrigation and investors will find this a profitable field for investigation."

## SHOSHONE COUNTY.

| | Assessment values. |
|---|---|
| Cœur d'Alene Railway & Navigation Company | $182,150 |
| Washington & Idaho Railway Company | 192,725 |
| Ditches | 60,000 |
| Telephone company | 2,600 |
| Patented land | 13,404 |
| Unpatented land | 20,000 |
| Improvements on above | 450,000 |
| Improvements on mining claims | 100,000 |
| Telegraph lines | 1,600 |
| 4 quartz-mills | 22,000 |
| 10 concentrators | 304,000 |
| 1 sampler | 8,350 |
| 2 smelters | 2,500 |
| Money | 50,000 |
| 109 beef cattle | 2,650 |
| 235 stock cattle | 3,525 |
| 170 American cows | 5,100 |
| Farming utensils | 2,000 |
| Fixtures | 10,000 |
| Franchises | 11,000 |
| Goods, wares, and merchandise | 237,000 |
| Harness, robes, and saddles | 1,000 |
| 38 tons of hay | 760 |
| 129 hogs | 800 |
| 112 horses at $90 | 10,080 |
| 384 Spanish horses, at $30 | 11,520 |
| Jewelry and plate | 2,000 |
| Law library | 1,000 |
| Lumber | 10,000 |
| Machinery | 60,000 |
| 30 mules, at $75 | 2,250 |
| Musical instruments | 3,100 |
| 5 oxen | 200 |
| Pianos | 3,050 |
| 75 sewing machines | 1,500 |
| 450 common sheep | 900 |
| 63 wagons and vehicles | 3,045 |
| 1,700 cords of wood | 3,400 |
| Other property not enumerated | 280,892 |
| Total valuation | $2,096,161 |

That portion of Shoshone county lying west of the Bitter Root Mountains and north of the summit of the range dividing the St. Joseph River from the Cœur d'Alene River, and extending to the easterly line of

Kootenai county, comprises what is known as the Cœur d'Alene mining country, which has become famous throughout the entire country for its mineral products. It is heavily timbered with pine, tamarack, and cedar, and traversed by splendid mountain streams, affording unlimited water-power for all purposes in connection with the treatment of ores.

In the six years since the original discovery of gold in this section its growth has been marvelous, and the camp now contains upwards of eight thousand people. The gold mining is almost entirely confined to the North Fork of the Cœur d'Alene River, which traverses this section, and its tributaries, Eagle, Pritchard, and Beaver creeks.

During the last six years the placer mines on these creeks have produced upwards of $2,500,000 in placer gold, although the mines have been worked only by small parties of men working with primitive implements and old-time methods. During the last year, however, there have been put in operation upon Pritchard and Eagle Creeks hydraulic mining plants, representing an investment of upwards of $200,000, which have been most successfully operated, and have realized the investors profits far beyond their expectations. The mountains on either side of these gulches are covered with what is called "old wash," being deposits of gravel, probably prehistoric river channels, in which large quantities of gold are found. The attention of capital and labor is now being largely directed toward these old river channels, and the waters of the neighboring lakes and rivers are being conducted to such points as will enable their richness to be fully tested and developed.

In the midst of these extended placer fields there are also many valuable quartz gold mines, some of which have been extensively opened and worked, and have been steady producers of gold bullion during the past year, yielding a product of upwards of $100,000, and with increased facilities for treatment of the ores will add largely to this yield in the coming year.

There are three stamp mills on Pritchard Creek and several arastras engaged in crushing and treating the ores from these mines. In addition to these mines that have been already opened, there are many valuable prospects that need only the capital and labor necessary to develop them to place them in the list of producing and profitable mines.

This wide region of mountain and gulch, covered with dense growths of pine, tamarack, and cedar, was comparatively unknown until five years ago, when the discovery of placer gold by Pritchard and his associates in the gulch now bearing his name excited the stampede which quickly populated the north and south forks of the Cœur d'Alene River with from 4,000 to 5,000 hardy men. In 1884 the first discovery of galena was made on Cañon Creek, a tributary of the South Fork, and the Tiger and the Poorman mines then located have since become famous for the volume and value of their product, and are now the nucleus of the flourishing town of Burke. Soon after was discovered the Bunker Hill and Sullivan mines on Milo Gulch, also a tributary of the South Fork, about twelve miles below the mouth of Cañon Creek. This last find was of such extraordinary magnitude and richness as to awaken the interest of Montana capitalists in the country, and the ensuing year they constructed a narrow gauge railroad from Lake Cœur d'Alene to these mines, and began hauling their ore to the concentrating works at Wickes, Mont. This was the entering wedge which opened the marvelous treasures of the Cœur d'Alene to the world, and enabled it in less than three years to become what it is to-day, the greatest lead producing region of the United States.

The development and working mines of the Cœur d'Alene at the present time are mainly on the South Fork and its tributaries. There are ten concentrators, of an average capacity each of 100 tons daily, now in operation along this line. Three of them, the Bunker Hill and Sullivan, the Emma and Last Chance, and the Stemwinder, being at Wardner. On Cañon Creek there are five: The Poorman, the Tiger, the San Francisco, the Gem and the Granite; while the town of Mullen, five miles west of the Montana line, has two, the Hunter and the Morning. These mills produce 70,000 tons of concentrates per annum, containing an average of thirty ounces of silver and 60 per cent of lead, to which must be added not less than 45,000 tons of selected ore sacked and shipped from the mines, averaging forty ounces of silver and 60 per cent of lead; and this entire output, aggregating a cash value of $9,030,000 at the market sale of ninety cents for silver and four cents for lead averages the mine-owners of the Cœur d'Alene, over all expenses of freight, treatment and percentage of loss, a clear profit of from $25 to $30 per ton; and the present development of other properties on the same mineral belts assure the belief that another two years will double the number of mills and production of ores and concentrates.

Along the South Fork, in consequence of this great output of mineral wealth, have grown a number of beautiful and flourishing towns, some of which will quickly assume metropolitan proportions with the completion of the railroads now building, and which by the shortening of distance and the unusually attractive and picturesque features of the county, will bring much of the transcontinental travel through the valleys of the Cœur d'Alene, and at the same time afford such increased facilities for transportation as will greatly increase the product of the mines now operating, and encourage the full development of the thousand valuable mineral prospects now lying dormant.

The North Fork of the Cœur d'Alene River and its tributaries are not less valuable and promising in mineral prospects, and a branch line of the Washington & Idaho Railroad is now located from the main line at Kingston to the head of Beaver Creek. It will undoubtedly be built next year for a distance of thirty miles. There it will tap the product of what is known as the Sunset Group of mines, a galena deposit of such magnitude as warrants the estimate now made of an output of not less than 700 tons per day from present developments. From the mouths of Beaver and Pritchard Creeks the North Fork trends to the north for about twenty miles, and heads in the southerly slope of the Cœur d'Alene Mountains, opposite Lake Pend d'Oreille. It is an unexplored region, but the few adventurous prospectors who have penetrated its pathless forests have brought out many specimens of mineral equal in richness to any yet found in the country, and it is believed from this and from its geological formation and position that when the Upper North Fork is thoroughly explored it will prove as prolific of wealth as any other mining district of the Cœur d'Alene.

Pritchard Creek, which empties into the North Fork about two miles above the mouth of Beaver Creek, runs for about fifteen miles through the gulch containing the immense placer deposits which first attracted attention to the country. Over $2,000,000 has been gathered from this ground by scattered and occasional labor on the rim rock and in shallow gravel, by small parties of men working with primitive implements and old-time methods; but all attempts to reach the bed-rock depths of the main gulch and the bottom of the Old Wash channel stretching for miles along the hills, were failures, and they remained untouched until two years ago, when a company of New York capitalists, after a long and careful expert exploration of the ground, and after securing mining claims of twenty acres each for miles, began the construction of an extensive bed-rock flume on one of the side gulches of Eagle Creek, which is tributary to Pritchard. Early last spring, with all of the latest appliances to hydraulic power, and with every known improvement to the methods of catching gold, they began work which resulted this fall in a sum total so far beyond all expectations that they are now preparing for the construction of a substantial and expensive system of flumes and ditches, with the view of a steady pursuit of this profitable work as their permanent business investment for years to come.

Another company of Eastern men are now investigating the prospect for a more extensive enterprise of like character along the main channel of Pritchard Creek, requiring a bed-rock flume of more than eight miles in length; and there is no doubt that during the coming year, with these and other organized efforts by men of means, the vast but stubborn placer fields of the North Fork will be compelled to give up their golden store.

### TOWNS OF SHOSHONE COUNTY.

The town of Wallace, with a population of 878, is situated in a beautiful basin of the South Fork Valley at the junction of Nine Mile, Placer, and Canon creeks, and is the supply depot of the great mining interests of these gulches. It is the railroad transfer for all the tributaries of the Upper South Fork, and has many well-supplied and substantial business houses in every branch of trade. It has two first-class hotels, several societies, good schools, and an able and enterprising tri-weekly paper, *The Wallace Free Press*. Wallace will more than double its population during the coming year from the fact of its selection as the division terminus of the through railroad now building toward Missoula, Mont.

Mullan, seven miles east from Wallace, has a natural location of great beauty, and is one of the coming towns of Cœur d'Alene. It is well built, has two fine hotels, a public school, and a weekly newspaper. *The Mullan*

*Tribune,* This promising place has a population of about 800, and is the center of a mining district equal in extent and richness to any in the country.

Wardner, in Milo Gulch, about two miles from the South Fork, is the business heart of the great group of working mines which have gradually opened in that district since the first discovery of the famous Bunker Hill and Sullivan. It is a flourishing town of 800 people, with schools, societies, fire department, and an excellent weekly mining journal and newspaper, *The Wardner News.* Its present population will largely and quickly increase when the railroad now building affords transportation for the full output of its mines.

The town of Burke, on Canon Creek, nine miles from the South Fork, has about 700 population, mainly supported by the Tiger and Poorman mines. It has a first-class hotel, water-works, fire department, and schools.

About four miles below in the same cañon is the town of Gem, with 200 people, around the newly-started works of the Gem and San Francisco mines.

At the mouth of Milo Gulch, two miles below Wardner, are the towns of Milo and Wardner Junction with an aggregate population of 500. Both of these places are enterprising business points, deriving their main support from the Wardner group of mines.

The town of Kingston, at the junction of the North and South Forks of the Cœur d'Alene River, has about 200 residents.

During the year 1890 there have been discovered, in addition to the gold mines, valuable deposits of galena ores near the town of Raven, at the head of Pritchard Creek, which, although only discovered during the summer, have already begun to ship their ores to market, and promise fair during the next year to be large producers. A correspondent says:

"The great reputation of this country, however, has been based upon the product of its lead-silver ores, which are found principally upon the South Fork of the Cœur d'Alene River and its tributaries, Milo, Nine Mile, and Cañon Creek. On these gulches there are upwards of thirty mines thoroughly developed and steadily producing silver-lead ores, which yield an average of about 30 ounces of silver per ton and 60 per cent of lead. A portion of the ores from these mines is of a character that can be shipped to the smelters without preliminary treatment, while a greater portion of it is what is called concentrating ores, or ores that by the concentration are reduced about 3½ or 4 tons into 1, and these mines produce about 90,000 tons of concentrates per annum, and about 65,000 tons of selected ore of the quality above named.

"There are in operation in this part of the camp eleven concentrators of an average capacity each of 100 tons daily. The value of the ores produced from these mines, with silver at $1.15 per ounce and lead at $5.75, will aggregate to the mine owners over all expenses of freight, treatment, and percentage of loss, a clear profit of from $45 to $55 per ton. And from the present development of other properties on the same mineral belts it is safe to predict that in another year the products of these mines will be increased by one-half."

In addition to this section of the camp are the mining properties on Sunset Mountain, lying midway between the North and South Forks, which have not yet been reached by railroad facilities, but which have in sight sufficient bodies of ore, well developed, to insure an increase of the product of the entire camp by at least one-half as soon as the facilities for transporting these ores to market are complete.

Two lines of railroad traverse this county from east to west, giving it direct communication with the outside world over both the Union Pacific and Northern Pacific railroads. Along the South Fork of the Cœur d'Alene River, in consequence of these great deposits of mineral wealth, have grown a number of beautiful and flourishing towns, some of which are now assuming metropolitan proportions, and which, because of the shortening of distances and the unusually attractive picturesque features of the country, will bring much of the transcontinental travel into the valleys of the Cœur d'Alenes, and the railroads now afford such increased facilities for transportation as will greatly increase the products of the mines, and encourage the full development of the thousand valuable mineral prospects now lying dormant. These mines are located in groups over a section of the country about 25 miles square, and near each group of developed mines there has grown up a flourishing mining town.

Murray, the county seat of Shoshone county, in which this mining camp is located, is on Pritchard Creek, about six miles from its junction with the North Fork of the Cœur d'Alene River. It is in the heart of the gold belt, and is surrounded with the gold-bearing quartz leads and placers referred to.

The town has a population of about 700, chiefly supported at present by the placer diggings and quartz mines in its vicinity. It has a public water supply, fire department, a lodge of the Masonic Order, and one of the Ancient Order of United Workmen, and a flourishing post of the Grand Army. It has also a lively weekly newspaper, the Cœur d'Alene *Sun*, and has a future of unquestionable and permanent prosperity.

## WASHINGTON COUNTY.

| | Assessment Values. |
|---|---:|
| Improved land patented, 48,022 acres | $ 463,520 |
| Improvements on above | 92,715 |
| Mining claims | 16,500 |
| Oregon Short Line Railway Company | 182,650 |
| Telegraph lines | 1,985 |
| 2 quartz mills | 12,000 |
| 1 smelter | 1,000 |
| 1 mining ditch | 3,000 |
| 3 irrigating ditches | 5,400 |
| Money on hand | 1,400 |
| 7,000 stock cattle at $11.50 | 90,850 |
| Farming utensils | 5,400 |
| Furniture | 6,600 |

|                                                        | Assessment Values. |
|--------------------------------------------------------|-------------------:|
| Goods, wares and merchandise                           | $ 24,750           |
| Harness, robes and saddles                             | 3,000              |
| 3,000 hogs at $4                                       | 12,000             |
| Mercantile establishments                              | 2,400              |
| 3 thoroughbred horses at $400                          | 1,200              |
| 5,000 graded horses at $25                             | 125,000            |
| 25 mules at $40                                        | 1,000              |
| Machinery                                              | 5,000              |
| Musical instruments                                    | 2,556              |
| 30,000 common sheep at $2                              | 60,000             |
| 450 wagons and vehicles                                | 4,500              |
|                                                        |                    |
| Total valuation                                        | $1,124,406         |

While this county has not advanced as rapidly as its friends desired and expected, yet it can truly be said that it has never lost a step once gained. The great value of its mines has been conceded by experts from every part of the country; the Seven Devils copper district has a continent-wide reputation, and new mineral discoveries are made year by year.

The agricultural resources of this county are confined, so far as developed, to the valley on the east bank of Snake River and the valleys of Weiser River and its tributaries. The former is twenty-eight miles long, through which runs the Oregon Short Line Division of the Union Pacific Railway, with depot at Weiser, and for this twenty-eight miles it will average three miles in width. Most of this land lies so high that it will not produce crops without irrigation. When irrigated it proves very productive and is adapted to all kinds of grain (including corn) and every kind of fruit and berry grown in the temperate zone. No ditches have been taken from Snake River to irrigate these lands. What irrigation has been done is from the waters of the Payette and Weiser rivers and at this date the ditches are not of sufficient capacity to irrigate more than one-twentieth of the land.

It is true, however, that the Weiser will not any season afford sufficient water to irrigate all the land, unless a system of storage is adopted. This river runs through the entire length of the county for about 100 miles or more, and its beautiful, fertile valleys from their shape would seem to have been a chain of small lakes at some time. They are named, commencing at the mouth of the river as follows: Lower Weiser, Middle Valley, Salubria, Indian Valley, Council Valley, and the Meadows. They vary little in size.

These valleys during the growing season require less irrigation as you ascend the river, and even in very dry seasons fine crops have been raised in Salubria Valley and the Meadows without irrigation. In the latter valley, the highest on the stream, a peculiarity exists that is worth mentioning. It is found that the earth is warmer than the surrounding air, as grass will be found growing under the snow, and as fast as the snow melts away grass from four to six inches long is seen, and from this fact the people living in the valley give it as a reason that their vegetables are not blasted by the frosts as in other valleys lying below them. There is not much grain raised in this county, for the reason that there is no profit in it in the upper valleys on account of the wagon transportation required to get it to any outside market, and the lower valleys have an insufficient water supply for irrigation. There were a few car-loads of wheat and barley shipped out of the county last year, but it is doubtful if any will be shipped this year, as much of the acreage sown to grain was cut for hay. The mines being as yet undeveloped, the home market for agricultural products is very limited. As a consequence the farmers convert their grain and hay into such products as will bear long transportation. Several car-loads of horses have been shipped this season.

Many are turning their attention to raising hay exclusively, and for this purpose alfalfa is taking the lead of all other grasses. There are only two flouring-mills in the county, one at Weiser and one at Salubria. Mr. John Cuddy, the owner of the last named, has machinery on the way to convert it from the burr to the full roller process. Considerable attention is now being paid to raising fine horses. A Mr. Thompson, of The Dalles, Oregon, has purchased a tract of land a few miles above the town of Weiser, and at considerable expense is fitting it up with stables and track to fit his horses for the turf. He has now at his stables some of the finest blooded horses in the West. Quite a number of Percheron stallions (some ten or fifteen) have been brought into the county and sold the past year. The tributaries of the Weiser River are settled to quite an extent, the same being from one to two farms wide along the streams and from five to fifteen miles long. Most of them produce fine crops, and a few are set to fruit and berries and supply the home demand. There are a number of hot springs in the county.

The agricultural towns of the upper portion of Washington are quite prosperous. Salubria is becoming a handsome and well ordered place. The farmers have thrashed 245,680 bushels of wheat this year, 150,000 bushels of oats, and 20,000 bushels of rye. They have raised 40,000 bushels of potatoes and proportionate amounts of other vegetables. They have stacked 83,000 tons of hay. The water system is constantly being enlarged and perfected, so that agriculture is beyond the accidents of drouth and storm.

The county has four flouring mills capable of producing 250 barrels of flour per day. It has twelve saw-mills, which cut 2,000,000 feet of lumber his year, and four shingle-mills, which cut 180,000 shingles. There are two quartz-mills and two smelters in Washington county; 20,000 tons of gold ore, and 10,000 tons of silver ore have been marketed. The production of silver is estimated at $100,000; gold, $25,000, and copper, $22,500.

Weiser, the county seat, has shared the general prosperity of the State of Idaho. The county authorities have provided a new court house at a cost of $16,000; the Weiser public school building has been completed at a cost of $7,000, and the Odd Fellows' hall cost $7,000. New additions have been platted and many intelligent men have invested liberally in this place.

This is the railway freighting and distributing point for a district 75 miles broad and 150 miles south to north. The altitude of Weiser is but 2,340 feet above sea-level. It is a handsome, healthful, and prosperous town of 901 inhabitants. It has many tasteful residences and substantial business houses and is the center of a fruit-growing district of great promise.

The town is incorporated and has an active board of trade, to which inquirers are advised to apply for detailed information.

## MINING.

In common with every mountain county in the State, Washington has her valuable mines, containing gold, silver, copper, and lead. They are but partially developed, and until within the last three years were not much thought of. They are now gradually coming into prominence, and bid fair to rival the best in the State. At the present time there are three mining districts, viz: Washington, Heath, and Seven Devils.

Washington district comprises the following silver lodes, which are now attracting attention: Black Hawk, Black Maria, Daniel Boone, Egan Group, Traveler, Muldoon, Kit Carson, Atlanta and some others, which are very little more than prospects. Those named have been partially developed, and for the amount of labor done show as much ore in sight as any mines in the United States. The valuable minerals of this district are silver, copper, and iron. The principal claims are taken upon lodes carrying silver, and are located in the vicinity of a mining town named Mineral. The lodes may be briefly described as a system of nearly parallel veins, whose strike is a little north of east, and whose dip, which varies from 30 to 70 degrees, is toward the north. Northeast they vary from two feet or less in thickness to twenty or even thirty feet. The grade of the ore, although generally esteemed low, is not so when compared with other silver camps. The concentrating ore being the undecomposed sulphurites in a porphyritic gangue are very abundant, and average twenty ounces per ton. Much of the oxidized vein matter will produce from thirty to forty ounces of silver to the ton.

There are three quartz-mills in the district, of a daily capacity of thirty-five tons, and one smelter of thirty-five tons capacity. Two of the mills named have been erected this season; one on the Daniel Boone, by Biddle & Lang, and the other on the Egan Group, by a company formed in Portland, Oregon. The population of the district is now about 200, a majority of whom are employed in or about the mines last above named.

HEATH DISTRICT.—The lodes of this district are large, well defined veins, carrying little if any valuable minerals except silver. The ores are of a lower grade than those of Washington district and far more rebellious in character; all have to go through the roasting process to be worked successfully. The names of the claims developed sufficiently to determine that they are true mines are the Belmont, Greenhorn, Buckeye, Climax, Hercules, Mary Ellen, and El Dorado. There is a ten-stamp mill on the Belmont, owned by the Heath Mining Company. They have expended not less than $75,000 on the mill and mine. There are two other small mills in this district that might be termed prospecting mills, although one has a roaster and amalgamating pan attached. The name of the camp where the mines are located, as also the post office, is Ruthburg. The population is about twenty.

SEVEN DEVILS DISTRICT.—This, the greatest mineral belt of the Nineteenth Century, was first discovered by Levi Allen, about twenty-five years ago, and at that time, he located what is known as the Old Peacock the phenomenal surface mine of the world. The name is derived from seven jagged, rough, inaccessible peaks, just north of the camp, which frown down upon it as though forbidding man to touch the treasures below. Allen had every confidenc♦ in its most wonderful value, and every year traveled nearly two hundred miles, fifty miles of this over a rough mountain trail; and alone, far from the haunts of men, in this secluded mountain dell, he did his assessment work as required by law. And here, entirely alone, $30,000 to $40,000 in gold was taken from the gulches around the great Peacock Lodge. And at a later day, J. Cooper chipped off a piece of ore carrying free gold which he sold for $20.

A new town called Helena has recently been platted and a post-office established, and Moses Fuchs appointed postmaster. The town site is located on a level bench and contains only twenty acres, as more land could not be secured on account of the rough and uneven nature of the district.

The town has a very thrifty appearance, though this would follow almost as a matter of course, as it is located within one hundred yards of the Old Peacock mine, which is conservatively estimated to have seventy-five thousand (75,000) tons of 35 per cent copper ore in sight. There is on the dump, sacked and being shipped, five hundred (500) sacks of ore that will average 42 per cent copper per ton. Twenty per cent copper ore will pay. Ten carloads of ore shipped the past season of 1890 averaged 40 per cent copper per ton, the highest going 47¾ per cent and the lowest (only one car) 32½ per cent. The Old Peacock, White Monument, Blue Jacket, Copper Crescent, Mountain Queen, Legal Tender, Helena, Calumet and Norma, are all patented mines and were recently sold by Messrs. Albert Kleinschmidt and Samuel Hauser of Helena, Montana, to a syndicate for $1,600,000 cash besides a large block of stock, and are now incorporated under the name of the American Mining Company, and capitalized at $5,000,000; John C. Rogers being the resident manager.

The pay streak in the Alaska is five feet wide and averages 40 per cent copper, 30 ounces in silver and $20 gold per ton. There is an incline down 45 feet on the vein and a tunnel in 100 feet. About 60 tons of ore on the dump. Col. E. H. Mix and others, of Baker City, Oregon, own this great property, and Geo. A. Ralm, of Weiser, Idado, has it bonded.

The Mountain King has an open cut 20 feet, showing a three-foot pay streak which averages from 50 to 60 per cent copper per ton, and 30 ounces in silver.

Three hundred tons of high grade copper ore have been shipped from the Mountain Queen this season. Average value per ton, 45 per cent copper, 20 ounces in silver and $10 in gold.

The Blue Jacket has a shaft down 145 feet (the deepest in the district) and the pay streak in the vein is from four to eight feet wide.

The Helena has 100 tons of ore on the dump and one tunnel is in 100 feet and shows a well defined eight-foot vein, all the way, of 45 per cent copper ore.

The Circle C and Triple X are big mines, owned by Moses Fuchs and Chas. Morris.

The Decoro is owned by Col. E. H. Mix, and Mr. Steele of Portland. A tunnel has been driven 75 feet on the vein and shows 250 tons of ore. On the dump 50 tons of 35 per cent ore.

About 10 tons of rich ore on the dump at the Arkansaw, and the 60-foot tunnel all in ore.

The Calumet has a tunnel in 30 feet and a shaft down 25 feet, and the pay streak three feet wide.

The Lockwood Group consists of the Lockwood, Lookout and Pomeroy. The Lockwood has a tunnel in 145 feet and a shaft 45 feet, which shows ore all the way that will average 40 per cent copper. About 50 tons of ore on the dump. .

The Dora is the property of Mrs. Jno. C. Rogers; the ore high grade and shows free gold.

The Sampson has a 100 foot tunnel, and the pay streak is 15 feet wide of low grade ore.

On the White Monument a tunnel has been run 100 feet, and 500 sacks of ore were shipped last year. This season, 600 sacks of 50 per cent copper ore were shipped. Many very rich and exceedingly handsome specimens of copper ore, showing great chunks of ore bound together by ropes of gold, have been taken out and all the ore goes high in gold.

The Copper Queen has shipped 1,600 sacks of fine ore this season.

The South Peacock is owned by a Boston syndicate, and shows a large well defined vein of high grade copper ore, showing much free gold.

The Copper Key was recently purchased by Boston people from Al. Donart and R. E. Lockwood; consideration, $20,000.

The only route to this wonderfully rich region is via the Union Pacific System, the equipment of which is unsurpassed, service excellent.

At present one must leave the Union Pacific at Weiser, Idaho, and thence 100 miles by stage or private conveyance to Helena, the only town in the great Seven Devils Mining Region. The town is only four miles from Snake River in a direct line, and a railroad grade eighteen miles long has already been made, and it is proposed to lay the track and ship all ores and supplies by rail to the head of navigation on Snake River, and thence by steamer to Huntington, which place is also on the Union Pacific.

The town site of Helena is less than half a mile from the old Peacock, South Peacock, Copper Key, Alaska, White Monument, Dora, Helena, Copper Queen, Crescent and other mines, all of which show large bodies of high grade gold, silver and copper ore. A population of at least 5,000 is confidently predicted during 1891.

## WILL IT PAY TO FARM?

Will it pay to farm in Idaho, and if so, how much? The question has been asked elsewhere, as well as here, and has been successfully answered. "What man has done, man can do," is a familiar motto. Here is the result of one farmer's operations:—

| | |
|---|---:|
| Interest on 160 acres of land, $10 per acre, at 10 per cent.................. | $160 00 |
| Water right, $800; interest on same.......................................... | 80 00 |
| Plowing, at $1.25 per acre.................................................... | 200 00 |
| Harrowing, 50 cents per acre................................................. | 80 00 |
| Seed wheat................................................................... | 150 00 |
| Labor of irrigation.......................................................... | 160 00 |
| Labor—harvesting and stacking............................................... | 400 00 |
| Labor—threshing—4,800 bushels............................................... | 384 00 |
| Marketing.................................................................... | 150 00 |
| Total expense................................................................ | $1,764 00 |
| Yield, 30 bushels per acre, 4,800 bushels, at $1 per bushel................. | $4,800 00 |
| Less expense................................................................. | 1,764 00 |
| Net profit, exclusive of labor, over all expenses................... | $3,036 00 |

As Government land can be had free on homestead, or as low as $1.25 per acre on pre-emption claims, the $160 interest money can often be carried to profit account, showing a still larger return. In sections of Northern Idaho, where irrigation is not absolutely required, there is the interest on the water right, and the cost of irrigation to be also added. This is for about eight months in the year.

Wheat is the least profitable of Idaho crops. The product of vegetables, hay, or fruits pays far better.

It is not unusual for immigrants to locate on wild land in Idaho valleys adjacent to mining regions, put up comfortable houses, good fences, etc., and pay for all such improvements with the first year's crop of potatoes or other vegetables taken from only a small portion of their farms. The facts that Idaho farmers were, as a rule, very poor when they embarked in business a few years ago, and that they are now generally well off and have fine buildings and the best implements, with often large herds of stock, are proof that this is a lucrative pursuit.

Idaho potatoes sell for 75 cents to $1 50 per 100 pounds—sometimes in mining camps much higher—and other vegetables in proportion. Take here in connection with grain raising, the production of poultry, eggs, butter, pork, vegetables, and similar items now almost unnoticed as "not worth bothering about," and the industrious and frugal farmer and housewife, managing as do those in thickly-settled States from necessity, should soon make themselves independent. It is often almost impossible in the winter to secure fresh eggs at 50 cents per dozen in Idaho towns, and during the past winter we have seen 75 cents offered. Butter often ranges from 40 to 50 cents the entire winter, and it is frequently impossible to secure a good article.

The constant increase in the magnitude of railway, mining, and other operations in all parts of the State justifies the belief that any considerable surplus of produce can not be raised in the mountain districts for years to come, and until that time prices must remain from 50 to 100 per cent higher than in the States. Again, agricultural land is usually so beneficently interspersed with the great mineral belts that the market will be at hand, and the miner accommodated as well as the farmer. This reminds us that in Pocahontas Valley, near the Oregon Short Line, there is a 160-acre homestead from one end of which fifty bushels of wheat per acre was harvested last season, while from a gulch at the other end gold was being mined to the extent of 50 cents per pan.

## FRUIT CULTURE.

Idaho valleys can not be excelled by any region east of California for the production of fruit. Apples, peaches, pears, nectarines, apricots, plums, grapes, and all small fruits are produced in the greatest abundance, and of a quality unsurpassed. The sage-brush lands, naturally the very emblem of sterility and desolation, are in a few years turned into the finest fruit farms with less trouble than would attend a similar transformation on the wild prairies of Iowa or Nebraska. A prominent fruit-grower estimates that 25,000 large fruit trees have been set out annually for the past five years in the valleys surrounding Boise City. Several of the orchards in this locality produce from 25,000 to 40,000 bushels of fruits each, annually. Gen. L. F. Carter, ex-Surveyor General of Idaho, has forty varieties of grapes in his vineyard, few of which have ever failed to bear a full crop, save the Catawba. John Krall, in the suburbs of Boise City, has 125 acres in fruits (20,000 trees), embracing all the varieties known in this latitude. The production of this fruit-farm in a recent season was 500,000 pounds. His market is mainly in the mining camps, and his fruits command from 3 to 10 cents per pound. Thos. Davis, also near Boise City, has a seventy-five acre orchard (10,000 trees). His orchard has failed to produce *but once in the last eleven years,* and his last season's crop of 40,000 bushels of large fruits and 500 bushels of berries returned him a snug little fortune alone. His orchard is eighteen years old. He irrigated the first four or five years, but has not found it necessary since. Mr. Davis has an extensive fruit-drying apparatus, and a cider vinegar factory, in which he works up vast quantities of fruit annually. Indeed, fruit-drying and the manufacture of cider is a prominent and very profitable industry. One firm dries from 30,000 to 40,000 pounds of fruit annually, and this industry bids fair to grow until at least the demand of Idaho and adjacent territory is supplied.

The fourth year's growth of apple trees in Boise Valley has yielded 200 pounds; of cherries, 75 pounds; peaches, 150 pounds; of pears, 130 pounds; of plums, 150 pounds; while small fruit, such as strawberries, currants, gooseberries, blackberries and raspberries, are very prolific. Many of the more elevated mountain regions, such as Wood River Valley, can duplicate these figures, except as to peaches. The growth of wood made by fruit trees, and the quantity of fruit often found loading the branches, is almost incredible. John Lamb, in Boise City, has black locust trees on which we were shown limbs that had grown from twelve to fifteen feet in one season, and plum, peach, and apple trees, two years from the graft, full of fruit. In another orchard we counted 140 nearly-ripe green gage plums on a branch seventeen inches long, the plums averaging one and a half inches in diameter.

Idaho is the very Eden for plums and prunes. The trees are perfectly healthy, grow vigorously, and bear much earlier than in the States east of the Rocky Mountains, and for size, beauty and excellence of flavor, the fruit is unsurpassed in any part of the globe. One farmer has sold his prune crop at an average of $600 per acre. Another has recently set twenty acres in prunes. Plums and prunes, especially the latter, are found to be so profitable for drying that many orchards are being planted for that purpose. There seems to be no danger of over-doing the business, as the plum and prune growing districts of the United States are very limited, and immense quantities of dried prunes are imported from Europe. The Idaho German prunes are pronounced superior to the imported fruit.

The "Fruit Belt" covers all the agricultural district in Idaho, although some elevated regions are too cool to admit of the production of peaches, apricots, and nectarines. In Wood River Valley, Camas Prairie, Bear Lake Valley, Malad Valley, Goose Creek Valley—all of which are really mountain valleys—all kinds of hardy fruits grow abundantly. Currants of a wild variety, when cultivated, grow as large as gooseberries, and gooseberries as large in proportion. In these mountain valleys the growth of these kinds of fruits is something remarkable. Strawberries and raspberries flourish and produce an excellent quality of fruit. Apples, pears, etc., have been grown sufficiently to insure their successful production. Many trees have been planted during the last three years, and several orchards are bearing slightly. The fruit is fair and free from worms. The trees that have been planted make a healthy and vigorous growth. It is known that cherries and plums will thrive, but winters are too severe for peaches.

There is a grand future in store for the Idaho fruit-grower. Montana to the north, Wyoming on the east, and Nevada to the south, produce practically no fruit. With her railroads, reaching the remotest corner of these States, and with a vast consumption at home, Idaho is assured the best fruit market in the land. Large shipments have already been made during recent seasons. Boise Valley has supplied not only her home market and Wood River, but also the neighboring territory with her fruits. Official figures show that out of a total of 500,000 pounds of fresh fruit received at Butte, Mont., up to November 1, 1887, 253,430 pounds were from Boise Valley, the remainder being from California, the Missouri River Valley, Utah and Portland. From November 1st, up to which date the above figures were given, an additional 150,000 pounds of apples were shipped to Butte from this valley, making in all 400,000 pounds of fruit contributed by Boise Valley to the single mining camp of Butte in one season.

A recent writer, in reference to the profits of fruit farm of Mr. Thomas Davis, near Boise City, says:—

"Preparatory to shipment, the apples are packed in fifty-pound boxes. They readily find a market in all parts of Idaho and adjoining States and Territories. No less than 250,000 pounds of this fruit have already been sent by rail to various parts of the Northwest, and Mr. Davis still has as many stored away in the three-story building, specially prepared for the purpose, and shipments continue to be made almost daily. Apples boxed and shipped net about $1.25 per 100 pounds, so we may safely calculate that the fruit already disposed of and that yet in store will bring Mr. Davis a clear $6,250. Besides this he has 150 barrels of vinegar, 20,000 pounds of choice dried apples, and a considerable quantity of pears and cider. Altogether this year, the net profit derived from this sample orchard will reach the handsome sum of $10,000. This is only a sample of what Idaho is doing in the way of producing fruit, which is everywhere pronounced of superior quality and delicious flavor."

As indicative to some extent of the long, mild growing seasons in the lower valleys of Idaho, we note the fact that the second crop of berries and other fruits is not infrequently picked the same year. Says the Boise *Statesman*, of October, 1888:—

"Dr. E. Smith showed us samples of a second crop of apples on one of the trees in his orchard. They were of the Early Bough variety, and were mellow and really good apples. Two peculiarities about these apples are worthy of mention. The first crop on the tree grew here and there all over the tree, while the second crop grew in clusters. In the first crop, the apples were round, and in the second, they were long and narrow. Strange freak this, all owing, no doubt, to this 'wonderful climate' of Idaho. F. II. McDonald, living near Star Postoffice, also brought to the *Statesman* office yesterday samples of a second and third crop of apples for the current year. The second-crop apples were large and mellow, really excellent eating apples, while the third crop were as large as walnuts with the shell on. They grew in bunches. We have seen a number of samples of second-crop apples, but this is the first we have seen of a third crop. Farmer McDonald may pass to the head of the class."

J. A. Goodhue, manager of the western branch of the Geneva Nursery, lately visited Western Idaho. In an interview he said:—

"I first went to Caldwell and stopped a number of days. The town has about 500 people, and is growing steadily. Merchants report business as satisfactory and all the time increasing. Produce brings good prices. Hay sells, I think, at $15 per ton; oats, $1.50 to $2 per 100 pounds; potatoes, $1 per 100; in fact, all products have a good market.

"I went along the Idaho Irrigating and Colonization Company's ditch. It takes water from the Boise River, opposite Caldwell, and extends northwest about twenty-three or twenty-four miles. It is completed, and is estimated to cover between 30,000 and 40,000 acres, all of which is first-class heavy sage-brush land. Most of this land is already taken, and quite a number are improving. I am having my section cleared of sage-brush, and the brush makes the fence. Such a fence is four feet wide and four and one-half feet high. Posts are put in a rod apart, and one strand of wire is stretched above. Such a fence will last a long time. Land can be cleared and fenced for about $4 per acre.

"I understand that arrangements have been made with Eastern capitalists to furnish money to buy the Ridenbough ditch, and to enlarge and extend it. This takes water from the river above Boise City and conveys it to the table-lands. After enlarging they will extend it to Nampa, thence to Bernad's and Henderson's Ferries. Its cost will be $100,000.

"I believe that part of Western Idaho extending from Boise City across south to Snake River and west to Weiser, will become the garden spot of Idaho within the next five years. I think Boise Valley the richest in Idaho. There is another locality a little farther east that should be mentioned, Mountain Home. The town is in the center of a large country subject to cultivation with irrigation."

## STOCK-RAISING.

The natural and long-continued dryness of the atmosphere—summer and winter—the almost inexhaustible and wonderfully nutritious grasses, which cure as they grow, making them as sustenance for animals, almost equal to the feeding of hay and grain, the infrequency of snow or other storms during the year, the warm breezes from the Pacific, and the ability of stock to live without shelter and take care of themselves, prove Idaho to be their natural home and breeding ground. Botanists inform us that on the 25,000,000 acres of Idaho grazing lands there are not less than thirteen different species of indigenous and nutritious grasses, all differing in leaf, height, root, and seed top, and which retain vigorous vitality throughout the coldest winters. The best and most common of these is the bunch-grass. It grows almost everywhere. There are several different varieties of bunch-grass, two of which are the most popular and generally known, one with a blade that resembles the blue-grass, and stems which run up in a cluster, bearing seed much in the same manner that blue-grass does, except that it does not form a tuft, but grows in bunches, and is found upon the high, rolling bench-lands, parks, and mountains. The other kind grows more frequently upon the first bench, next to the bottoms; the blade is sharp, the heads all turn to one side, and from the broad boot on the seed-stock is often called the "flag-grass." As to quantity per acre there is but little, if any, difference. The latter is usually preferable for cattle, but the former is thought to be best for sheep, yet either is very fine.

These grasses start forth in early spring and grow very rapidly. If there have been heavy snows during the winter, and the ground is well saturated with water, or if there are frequent rain and snow storms as the spring opens, the crop of bunch-grass is very large. In ordinary springs the grass is headed out by the 1st of June, and the prairies and hills, where not covered by sage, are beautiful as a waving field of grain. The height of the grass is usually from six to twelve inches, with blades from six to eight inches long; yet under very favorable circumstances it grows much taller. We have seen miles and miles of bunch lands along the mountain slopes, which were one vast sea of bunch-grass fully eighteen inches high and thick enough to mow. By the last of June the heads ripen, and in ordinary seasons the blades are all nicely cured by the middle of July, and the whole landscape is brown as a field of grain ready for the sickle, and would burn if set on fire. In exceptional seasons the blades of grass remain green and continue to grow until September. There is, however, no advantage in it remaining green, as there seems to be no perceptible difference in the fattening of stock. In fact, many incline to the opinion that the early cured is the best. The cured grass retains its nutriment all winter, from the fact that there are no drenching rains in the fall to bleach it, the light snows which come in early winter, and melt off soon, only serving to moisten it and make it more palatable. Then the shrubs, such as white, black, and yellow sage, and greasewood are abundant and invaluable for winter grazing.

There is an almost unlimited area of summer pasturage in the mountains and many mountain parks and elevated valleys, while the Great Snake River plains and tributary valleys have thus far afforded an ample winter feeding ground. This refers to the purely "range" cattle business, in which the animals are left wholly to care for themselves. In this way the annual expense of caring for cattle or horses of 1,000 or more, is about $1 per head. Adding taxes, and we have the total cost of producing a $30 steer—$4.50. Men, who five to ten years ago engaged in the business on a small capital, find themselves rich. The consequence is that many business men in recent years have invested in cattle. All figure on a profit of from 25 to 35 per cent per annum, Stock cattle, all ages and sexes, sell in Idaho at an average of about $18 per head. Until the country is thoroughly stocked, no money is needed for a ranch. Improvements generally consist of rough log huts and corrals, which, for say 1,000 head of cattle, need not cost over $250, if the owner relies largely on his own muscle. The additional expense is the cost of living, if the owner does his own herding, and this will vary from $250 to $400 a year. If a herder is employed he receives about $35 per month and board.

But the cattle business is rapidly taking a different, a more satisfactory, and equally profitable form. Owing to the rapid occupation of the ranges and their gradual reduction by the encroachment of farmers, many stock men are already securing tracts of the fertile Government land near their ranges and providing feed for at least a portion of their cattle. Herds are being rapidly improved by the introduction of blooded bulls of the best beef breeds. One breeder, near Hailey, has nearly 200 head of choice thoroughbred shorthorn cattle, which he shipped from Kentucky during the summer of 1888, in pursuance of this new plan. Fields of clover, alfalfa, and other grasses are being sown, to feed them a month or two in the winter, and it is estimated that within three years the average value of such herds will have doubled, thus amply justifying the additional expense and trouble. One hundred acres of clover or alfalfa, at a low estimate, will produce 500 tons of hay. This will, during the average Idaho winter, feed 500 head of cattle, keeping them in a fine, growing condition, absolutely insuring them against loss, and produce as much weight in a 3-year-old steer as the 4-year-old would weigh under the old system.

There is a grand field for the investment of either large or small capital in either of these systems. In Bingham, Lemhi, Washington, Alturas, Owyhee, and Ada counties, and all along the Snake River for 400 miles, in sight of the Oregon Short Line, as well as in Northern Idaho and Eastern Oregon and Washington, are vast and only partially occupied cattle ranges, where the fortunate few who are established are on a sure and short road to fortune. The present low price of cattle makes it possible for the new-comer to get his start in these districts under much more favorable circumstances than did the hundreds who have become comfortably "well off" during the past ten years in this business.

About 30,000 head of cattle are marketed annually, most of which are shipped over the Union Pacific Railway to Eastern markets, the balance being consumed in Idaho towns and mining camps.

Stock trains on the Union Pacific, from Idaho points eastward, are run on passenger train time, and the rates to Chicago are only a comparatively small advance over those from points much nearer the East. This accommodation and concession upon the part of the Union Pacific Railway Company, when taken in consideration with the superior natural advantages of this region, places the Idaho stock raiser in a very favorable position when compared with those east of the Rocky Mountains.

In a letter to the writer of these pages, Hon. George L. Shoup, Governor of Idaho, has this to say on the subject of stock-raising: "The stock grower is also rewarded with a handsome income from his herds of cattle, sheep, and horses. Cattle and horses winter in Idaho without hay or grain, subsisting and keeping in good condition upon bunch-grass, sweet sage and other nutritious food; a ready market at good prices is found in the mining camps for most of the beef produced, and the surplus is shipped to Chicago and other Eastern markets. The shipment can be made profitable on account of reduced rates given by the Union Pacific Railway from points on its Utah & Northern branch. From the writer's personal experience in cattle raising, he can verify the statement that it can be conducted with profit. Like all other kinds of business, a few have been disappointed in not realizing their expectations. The cause is easily traced to the fact that their stock was permitted to run at will, many of the increase going unbranded, much of the old stock wandering off to neighboring ranges, and in the fall of the year no care was taken to place the stock on a good winter range. Those having taken care of their stock have in all cases done well, and have made more money than could have been realized from the same amount of capital invested in any other legitimate enterprise."

Another old resident writes as follows: "The farmer and stock raiser have the endless mountain range, free of taxes, upon which to raise their stock. From the very nature of the country, there will always be comparatively few towns in Idaho. The real business will be farming, stock raising, and mining. While fortunes will be made for ages to come at the last-named business, stock raising and farming will be the most certain investments. Stock raising must always be good; for, as I said before, it costs but little to raise stock, and farming will always pay well, as the miners will consume all that will be raised in the valleys, and the produce will command higher rates than can be obtained in the States. I could pick out, here and there, all over the Territory, valleys that whole neighborhoods from the States could move into and find homes, which, in a short time, they would not exchange for their old ones. It is hard to tell which is more profitable here, raising cattle or horses, as I find a wide difference of opinion on the subject. It certainly takes less capital to start in the cattle business; but with capital to start on, I am inclined to believe raising horses and mules is the most remunerative. There are not many sheep here, but the business is a good one."

We have before us the statement of a stockman who commenced with $3,500, buying 100 head of cows, putting up a neat log cabin and reserving enough of the capital to pay his expenses for one year. At the end of the fourth year the increase from the little herd, at a low valuation, was worth $8,000. Another statement made for us by a well-known stockman, shows a net profit of $42,500 made in six years from an investment of $13,500. We are well acquainted with another prominent stock grower in Lemhi Valley, who invested $11,000 in cattle ten years ago. A year or two later he added $9,000 to his investment, mainly buying cows at the then high price of $40 per head. At the end of the first ten years he had sold enough of the increase to get back the $20,000 invested, as well as to pay all the expenses of carrying on the business for the ten years, and he has over $100,000 worth of cattle left. His loss last year was only 1 per cent, and it has averaged less than 3 per cent for years at a time.

Horses, more hardy than either sheep or cattle, because they will paw away the deepest snow that may cover their pasturage, are also being introduced in large numbers, despite the large amount of capital required for a respectable start. The average increase of colts is 80 per cent of the mares. No hay or grain is usually fed, except to the thoroughbred leaders of the herds, of which there are now quite a large showing. An authority on such matters estimates that there is room for 200,000 head of horses on Snake River Valley alone, where this industry seems to be taking the lead. There are at present, according to the official reports of the assessors, 123,804 horses in Idaho. A large proportion of these are native or "broncho" stock, although many herds of a better class are being established, and most of the ordinary herds are being readily improved by the introduction of good-blooded sires. One breeder spent $10,000 on the improvements of a 1,000-acre ranch near Hailey in 1888. He is stocking it with imported draft stallions and large native mares.

A correspondent offers these practical suggestions on this business: "What are wanted here are good draft-horses, and the market for such would be limitless at paying prices. Suppose a man, probably in connection with some other business, such as sheep raising or raising grain, were to buy fifty brood mares (half-breeds), which he can procure for $30 each, and one draft stallion, costing $1,000. He will thus have invested $2,500. He need be at no expense for feeding or stabling, except in the case of the stallion, and at very little expense for herding, if he gives the business his personal attention. The average of colts is 80 per cent of the mares, so that at the end of the first year he would have forty colts worth $20 each, making $800, a return of over 30 per cent on his investment. Carry this computation forward, and suppose him to sell off his geldings when they are four years old, to pay expenses and buy additional stallions, retaining the mare colts for breeders, and it will be seen that in five years he will have a herd worth at least $10,000."

## WOOL-GROWING.

Idaho is making rapid strides in wool-growing. From 50,000 sheep in 1880, her herds have increased to 350,000 in 1888. The profits of wool-growing are, by many, placed higher than in cattle-growing. All agree that the wool-clip will pay every item of expense, leaving the increase a clear gain. The annual increase of 1,000 ewes, two years old and upwards, will range from 85 to 115 per cent, while the increase of flocks of all ages and sexes is placed at 48 per cent. The loss from all causes is estimated by a majority of the prominent breeders with whom we have conversed, at 2 to 8 per cent. Few flocks are sheltered in winter, and but few receive any feed other than that gathered by themselves. Sheep raising is emphatically the poor man's industry, for, with a free range, timber at hand for shade and corrals, and, in fact, no capital needed for running expenses after the first season, he is master of the situation if he can command any sum from $500 upwards for the purchase of a small flock. Better still is the plan of leasing flocks, by which the trusty workingman without a dollar can secure a flock of from 1,000 to 2,000 head, for say five years, giving the owner one-half the increase and wool, and returning the original number of sheep at the termination of the lease. Many a poor man has become wealthy by starting in the business in this way.

One instance of this kind is noted near Caldwell, where a poor herder, with practically no capital but his muscle and energy, took 1,000 sheep on the shares, agreeing to return the original number of ewes in four years, with half of the total increase, and to deliver one-half of the entire wool-clip. In 1880, the increase was 1,050; in 1881, 1,250; in 1882, 1,400. In July, 1880, the owners received $650 for their half of the wool-clip; in 1881, $1,000, and in 1882, $1,100. The herd numbered 7,000 at the end of the four years, worth at least $22,000, and the wool-clip of the last year was worth $4,500. The owners thus had received in four years, $5,000 worth of wool and 3,000 sheep, worth $10,000, or a return of $15,000 in four years, from an investment of $4,000, and have their original band of sheep besides. The renter had not a dollar at the start, but has now a $20,000 flock of sheep and a well-improved ranch.

Robert Noble, whose flocks range near the Oregon Short Line, in Owyhee county, was thirteen years ago working for $30 a month. He invested a few years' wages in sheep, and is now accounted worth $150,000 to $200,000.

It needs no argument to prove that these high, dry localities in the Northwest are the natural home of the sheep. It is next to impossible to originate disease among sheep here, where they are out in the sunshine every day in the year, where there is no moisture to continually saturate the hoof and produce foot-rot, or to saturate the fleece and invite scab and other skin diseases. Browsing where it is never muddy, the fleeces rarely get dirty or matted, and while rarely washed before shearing, the wool is often as clean as that which is washed in most of the States.

Idaho sheep are being very rapidly improved. The average weight of fleeces four years ago was less than four pounds, while it is now six pounds.

Owing to the excellent railroad facilities and rates offered by the Union Pacific Railway, Idaho mutton is laid down in the Eastern markets at such good time as to afford the wool-grower a fine profit from his wethers. Eastern buyers always go to the wool-growers, and as the Idaho fleece is much sought after, there is practically a home market. About 2,000,000 pounds of wool were shipped from Idaho in 1888. One buyer of mutton sheep purchased 50,000 wethers at from $2.25 to $2.50 per head for shipment East from Idaho over the Union Pacific Railway during 1888.

Stock men reported cattle, sheep, and horses, doing remarkably well on Idaho ranges up to January 15, 1889. At that date Idaho was furnishing fat cattle for Portland, Seattle, Tacoma, and other Pacific Coast towns, and getting better prices than could be obtained in Eastern markets, whither all shipments were made prior to three months ago. Many thousand head of cattle were also shipped from Idaho to Montana ranges in 1888, where they had suffered a shortage on account of the previous severe winter. Idaho ranges have not suffered seriously on account of severe winters for many years, and are regarded as exceptionally reliable when compared with the more elevated States surrounding on the east, south, and north.

## DAIRYING.

A thousand dairymen are needed right now in Idaho. There are probably more and better openings for dairymen in that country than for any other branch of rural industry. The cattle king, with his thousands of cows, often either buys his butter or does without, and the denizens of cities, towns, and mining camps now look for the butter famine as regularly as winter comes. In winter a prime article of ranch butter is worth from 40 to 60 cents per pound, and will average 35 to 40 cents the year round. Climate, pasturage, and water combine to render dairying there a very satisfactory pursuit. Cows cost comparatively little for their keep, and the product of butter or cheese is a clear gain, the increase in stock paying expenses. Good dairy cows can be purchased at $35 to $45 per head.

In the center of the best grazing region in the world, with a superior climate, an abundance of clear, cold, running water, and whole "counties of grass" to be had for the taking, Hailey, Boise, and other Idaho cities send to other States for hundreds of thousands of pounds of butter and cheese annually. Haste the day when this grand region may be supplying its own demand, and sending its car-loads of butter and cheese East by express daily. What an advantage the dairyman of Idaho will have over his brother of the East! He can graze his cows on lands that cost him nothing, winter them at a cost of not to exceed $5 per head, and make and keep his butter and cheese in nice shape without the use of ice, while the dairyman of the East has $5,000 to $10,000 invested in every 100 acres of his pastures, expends $20 on every cow for winter keep, and suffers more or less annoyance and expense on account of the hot days and nights of his busiest season.

Idaho has hundreds of mountain parks and glens, each with its clear, cold streams winding through natural meadows, and its surrounding hillsides carpeted with the most nutritious grasses. Here is the ideal field for the dairyman. With cool nights, cold water, an atmosphere of perfect purity, free pasturage, the best markets in the world already developed—what more can be added?

Any of the branches of stock raising thus briefly outlined present opportunities without end for speedy money-making in Idaho. The requisites are in a nutshell—some capital at least, a careful study of the business, and the same attention devoted that would be bestowed upon any legitimate business venture of equal magnitude. So long as the world pays its greatest tribute to food—to bread and beef—the demand must ever keep its proportion beyond the supply, and these broad pastures and thousands of nestling valleys are ready and waiting to respond to the magic touch of labor and capital, judiciously applied.

## MANUFACTURING.

A grand field is open here for manufacturing enterprise. With water-power sufficient to turn the burrs and spindles of the world, inexhaustible quantities of iron, coal, copper, and other minerals, forests unexcelled, and wool, hides, ores, and other raw materials in any desired quantity, Idaho may well be investigated by those having capital and experience to expend on manufactures. With the exception of some two dozen saw-mills, and about the same number of flouring mills, this industry is almost wholly undeveloped in Idaho.

There is a production of over 2,000,000 pounds of wool from the rapidly increasing flocks of Idaho annually. From experiments made under similar conditions in neighboring States and Territories, woolen-mills can undoubtedly be made to pay in Idaho. A magnificent and unlimited water-power can easily be developed at the American Falls of Snake River, at a station of the same name on the Oregon Short Line. The vast volume of the river here has a descent of some fifty feet immediately under the railway bridge spanning the stream. Good openings, with ample water-power, are also presented to such an industry at Hailey, Boise City, Caldwell and other points.

There is not a foundry or machine-shop for 500 miles along the Oregon Short Line and Utah & Northern Railways, and several are needed. With coal, iron, zinc, lead, and all the other ores in the mountains, Idaho should be the metallurgist's, iron founder's, and machinist's own chosen country.

Thousands of hides from Idaho go East annually to be tanned, and returned for use at the points from whence they were originally shipped. The necessary bark and other adjuncts for successful tanning are plentiful and cheap. Several tanneries would find a profitable field in Idaho.

Abundant materials are found for pottery and the manufacture of glass, but both these articles are shipped from the far East. One institution engaged in bottling the famous Idanha mineral water at Soda Springs, Idaho, uses many car-loads of bottles annually.

As adjuncts to slaughter and packing-houses, stearine candles (used in the mines) and soaps should be made with much profit to the owners. There is one small soap factory at Caldwell.

More lumber-mills, planing-mills, and sash and door factories are needed. There is a large and constantly increasing demand for products of such factories, which are now largely shipped from distant States. The raw material of an excellent quality is practically inexhaustible.

Improved roller flouring mills are much needed at numerous points, among which Hailey, Caldwell, Payette, and Weiser present particularly favorable openings. Water-power is abundant at these points, and the supply of grain would be ample to employ mills of fair size    Idaho wheat is now, to some extent, shipped eastward and westward 300 to 500 miles, and then returned as flour.

No finer openings exist anywhere than that in the Boise and other valleys for the canning of fruits and vegetables. The choicest fruits and vegetables are produced, and train loads shipped to outside markets, while the consumption of canned goods shipped from California and the East aggregate many car-loads annually.

The reduction of precious metal ores presents a vast field for capital in Idaho. The districts in which various kinds of machinery could be introduced at an assured great profit are probably more numerous in Idaho than anywhere else in the world. The field is almost wholly new, and it is inviting to a wonderful degree.

## EDUCATIONAL ADVANTAGES.

The cause of education is keeping pace with the material development of the State. There are at present 337 school districts, with 365 schools, and 268 school houses costing an aggregate of about $350,000, and a school population (between five and twenty-five years of age) of 18,506. Expenditures for school purposes in 1888, were $138,662. The school system consists of a State Superintendent, County Superintendents, and District Trustees.

The general school law provides that all moneys accruing from the sale of all lands heretofore given, or which may hereafter be given by the Congress of the United States for school purposes, in said State, and all moneys that may hereafter be given and appropriated by the Congress of the United States for school purposes, unless the same by special provision shall be appropriated for the establishment of a university or other high school, together with any moneys by legacy or otherwise donated for educational purposes and appropriated to the general fund, and all moneys accruing to the State from unclaimed moneys from the estate of deceased persons, shall be set apart, and shall constitute an irreducible and indivisible State general school fund, the interest accruing from which only shall be appropriated to the respective counties of the State, in the manner hereinafter specified and directed.

For the purpose of establishing and maintaining public schools in the several counties in the State, it is the duty of the county commissioners of each county, at the time of levying the taxes for county and State purposes, to levy a tax of not less than two mills nor more than eight mills on each and every dollar of taxable property, in their respective counties, for school purposes.

The proceeds of fines and forfeitures, and certain licenses, also go to the County School Fund.

Boise City, Hailey, Bellevue, Ketchum Shoshone, and Lewiston each constitute an independent school district. Each has a graded school in every way creditable to the State. The Boise City building cost $50,000; that in Hailey, $30,000; and Bellevue. Shoshone. Lewiston, Ketchum, and Caldwell each have a building costing from $8,000 to $12,000. Religious, sectarian, and political doctrines are expressly forbidden to be taught.

Teachers' salaries vary according to locality and character of the school. In agricultural sections they range from $50 to $75 per month; in mining regions from $60 to $125, and in the larger towns from $65 to $150 per month.

The schools generally are better than could be naturally expected in so new a country. Great care is exercised in the selection of teachers, and the home-seeker coming to Idaho may be sure of finding abundant educational facilities in the elementary and graded schools of the State.

By the Act of February 18, 1881, Congress granted to the Territory of Idaho, seventy-two sections of public lands for school purposes, under certain restrictions. These, with the 3,000,000 acres of school lands (sixteenth and thirty-sixth sections) allowed under the general law, will undoubtedly at some future day form the basis of a sound, substantial school system.

By Act of the last Legislature every parent or guardian is required to send his child to school for at least twelve weeks in each school year, eight of which must be consecutive. This Act applies only to children between the ages of eight and fourteen years, and who reside within two miles of the school-house by the nearest traveled road. A failure to comply with the said law subjects the parent or guardian to a fine of not less than $5, nor more than $50. There are, under certain conditions, exceptions made in the law, and the board of trustees in each district are permitted to excuse the parents from complying with the provisions of the law. The Methodists, Presbyterians, Episcopalians, and Catholics have also established sectarian schools, and numerous private schools, some of a high grade of excellence, exist.

As one instance showing the growth in school matters in Idaho, the Superintendent of Public Instruction, in his report for 1888, says: "I find from the files of this office that in 1870 the total number of children of school age was only 888; we now have 20,130. In that year only $9,220.06 was spent for education, this year over $138,662.56 was expended. Then we had but 29 districts; now they number 337. Statistics may be deemed by many uninteresting, but the above seem to be convincing in proof that our school financial interests and population are marvelously increasing and must be provided for energetically."

## USEFUL MINERALS, ETC.

Besides her precious metals, Idaho also has an abundance of iron, coal, lead, copper, salt, sulphur, mica, marble, sandstone, granite, limestone, and some cinnabar, and tin. The State is, therefore, well equipped by nature for many industries besides those now engaging her attention. She has iron varied enough in kind and quality, and vast enough in quantity, for the uses of a great nation. Her copper ores are scarcely less abundant, and her coal fields, though but slightly developed, promise to meet all possible requirements in the near future.

IRON.—Near Rocky Bar is a seven-foot vein of ore, carrying 56 per cent pure iron. Within two miles of Challis is an immense body of micaceous iron, yielding 50 to 60 per cent of that metal. At several points along Wood River oxide ores, carrying 50 to 75 per cent iron are found in inexhaustible quantities. Near Baker City, along the Western Idaho boundary, are mammoth deposits of metallic iron, carrying 70 to 90 per cent of that metal. Three miles east of South Mountain, in Southwestern Idaho, is the Narragansett iron mine, where a surface of 100 by 600 feet of the vein has been stripped, and the limit not reached. A cut into this vein twenty feet deep and fifty feet wide, exposes a solid body of magnetic and specular ore, which numerous assays prove to contain 95 to 98 per cent pure iron  This ore is so pure and easily smelted that it has, in its natural state, been cast into shoes and dies for stamp mills at a Silver City foundry. A fifteen-foot vein of hematite, near by, is also rich in iron, and carries $30 per ton in gold. We have noted many other valuable deposits of iron in the State, among these several within a day's ride of Lewiston, in North Idaho, containing from 50 to 75 per cent iron.

COAL.—Bituminous coal is found in apparently inexhaustible quantities along Bear Lake, near the Southeastern Idaho boundary. It is said to be a fine quality for coking and for furnace use. The coal of the beds on Goose Creek, seventy-five miles south of Shoshone, in Southern Idaho, is pronounced by experienced geologists to be brown lignite, and similar to the famous German brown coal. It is of an excellent quality for heating, steam, and gas purposes. The beds, ten in number, vary in thickness from three and one-half feet to eighteen feet, and lie in two distinct series, with seventy-five feet to 100 of sandstone between. All the parting between the various veins is of sandstone, and rather hard, requiring no timbering in working. One of the beds, and one upon which the greatest amount of work has been done, is eighteen feet in thickness, with one small parting, showing a face of solid coal fourteen feet in thickness. Access to the region is easy from the Oregon Short Line. The carboniferous formation extends over an area of perhaps twenty miles square; the principal out-cropping besides those of the main beds on Goose Creek are to be found on Trapper Creek and on Grouse Creek, where a limited amount of fine coking coal has been found. Coal mines are open on Smith's Fork and on Twin Creeks, along the Oregon Short Line in Eastern Idaho, and the famous Mammoth mine shows a vein seventy feet thick of clear coal, and with adjacent veins, separated by thin veins of clay, will aggregate 200 feet in thickness. A good quality of lignite has been found near Boise, bituminous at Horse Shoe Bend, twenty-five miles from Caldwell, also between Payette and Weiser Rivers, forty miles from Caldwell, and at the Big Bend of Snake River, forty miles from Weiser. A good blacksmithing coal has also been found on Sucker Creek, twenty-two miles north of Silver City, and several large deposits near Lewiston, in Northern Idaho. None of these veins are worked to any considerable extent, because wood for fuel has been so plentiful and cheap, but the day is fast approaching when a good coal mine will be classed a bonanza in Idaho, by virtue of railway extension and the activity in mining and manufacturing enterprises.

COPPER.—St. Charles mining district, in the eastern edge of Idaho, near the Oregon Short Line, contains copper ore assaying 60 to 80 per cent, and native copper of great purity. The copper deposit can be traced for thirty-five miles. Along the southwestern edge of Camas Prairie, near Mountain Home, is an extensive network of copper veins, from one to six feet in thickness, their ores containing about 40 per cent copper. Near Brownlee's Ferry. forty miles north of Weiser, are several large veins running 60 per cent copper, and fifty miles farther north in the Seven Devils district, are great outcrops of peacock copper ore assaying 65 per cent copper and $25 in gold and silver per ton. There are many other copper deposits in Alturas and Custer counties.

LEAD.—Idaho is a great producer of lead. Wood River, Smoky, Bay Horse, Viola, Cœur d'Alene, and other districts are heavy shippers of lead ores, containing 50 to 80 per cent lead and $50 to $200 in silver to the ton. The Wood River mines alone ship from 20,000 to 30,000 tons of lead annually.

CINNIBAR occurs in nearly all the placer claims of Idaho county. At Miller's Camp, twenty miles west of Warren, it is found in such quantities as to prove troublesome in washing gold, filling the riffles where gold should lodge. Although the vein or lode has been persistently sought for, it has not been found. In one gulch pieces of iron ore containing from 10 to 50 per cent of gold have been found, but its source has not yet been traced. Thin ore has been observed in the same locality.

SALT.—About sixty miles northeast of Soda Springs, in a small side valley which opens into Salt Creek, near what is known as the Old Lander Emigrant Road, are the famous salt springs of Oneida county. No pumping is required, but the water is run through wooden pipes into large galvanized iron pans, in which the salt is made by boiling the water. The water is as cold as ordinary spring water, and is perfectly clear, showing how completely the saline matter is held in solution. The salt is shoveled out once in thirty minutes, and after draining twenty-five hours, is thence thrown into the drying house, there to remain until sacked and ready for shipping. The supply of water would warrant 2,500 pounds of salt per day. There is another small spring near by, which yields water enough for 2,000 pounds of salt per day for a portion of the year. The owners began to supply the local markets in 1866, at 5 cents per pound.

Following is the analysis of the Oneida salt made by Dr. Piggott, of Baltimore. ' It shows a higher percentage of pure salt than the celebrated Onondaga brand, of Syracuse, while neither Liverpool, Turk's Island, nor Saginaw salt approaches it in purity, or is as white, clear, or soluble in liquids:—

| | |
|---|---:|
| Chloride of sodium (pure salt) | 97.79 |
| Sulphate of soda | 1.54 |
| Chloride of calcium | .67 |
| Sulphate of magnesia | Trace |
| Total | 100.00 |

The increasing demand for salt from the smelting works of Idaho and Montana should in time, with improved transportation facilities, make the Oneida salt works of inestimable value. As it is, a very nice business has been done at these works, the product having for years been from 600,000 to 1,500,000 pounds per annum.

MARBLE.—Marble has long been known to exist in the valley of the Snake. The marble bluffs in the vicinity of the Bonanza Bar, sixteen miles below American Falls, have been known for years to furnish a good, marketable quality, but nothing was attempted toward its utilization until recently. The Union Pacific mineralogist and geologist some time ago took samples of the marble to Omaha, where it was found to be of a quality hardly second to the best Italian. Machinery will soon be put up for quarrying and sawing the marble and putting it in marketable shape  It is now being worked into monuments, etc., on a small scale, by a marble cutter, who ships it from Shoshone. Large deposits of white and variegated marble are found along the Clearwater, also in Kootenai and Cassia counties.

BUILDING STONE.—Granite and sandstone of the finest quality—white, pink, gray, and other shades—easily quarried and worked into any desirable shape, abound in various localities along the Oregon Short Line. In Nez Perces county, Northern Idaho, there is a quarry of sandstone of superior quality for making grindstones or other stones for sharpening edged tools.

LIMESTONE.—There are inexhaustible quantities of excellent limestone near Hailey, Boise, Weiser, and elsewhere, from which a superior article of lime is made.

SULPHUR.—There is a mountain of almost pure sulphur, running to 85 per cent of that useful commodity, at Soda Springs, Eastern Idaho. The sulphur has been mined and shipped in a small way for several years, while fifty miles of expensive wagon transportation was necessary, and now, with a railroad at hand, the enterprise should be pushed on a large scale.

MICA.—Forty miles north of Weiser, near Weiser River, are two ledges, eight by ten feet wide each, of mica. The mines are being developed, and thousands of tons of mica are now on their dumps. Clear, merchantable sheets, four by six inches in size, can be extracted in vast quantities. Deposits of mica are also known to exist near Pend d'Oreille Lake, and south of Lewiston, in Northern Idaho. Also at the City of Rocks, in what is known as "The Circle," fifty miles south of Shoshone, is a mica prospect, which is thought to be valuable. Sheets a foot in extent are obtained, which show a quality of mica which may prove to be of commercial value. It is tough and transparent.

BRICK CLAY.—Brick clay and potter's clay are plentiful in several localities. The manufacture of fine pressed brick is carried on at Hailey, Ketchum, and other points, and a good quality of deep red brick are made at almost every prominent point along the Oregon Short Line.

## FISHING AND HUNTING.

Idaho is the earthly paradise of the sportsman. As for trout, Idaho waters are simply alive with them. During thousands of miles of travel in the Idaho mountains in the fishing season, we can not say that we ever halted two nights where we could not catch a nice mess in an hour. They are so plentiful in different lakes and streams that they are caught by the wagon load for market. The real delicate, gamy mountain trout, weighing from a half pound to two pounds, and the salmon trout, affording just about as much sport and as fine eating, weighing from two to ten pounds, are often found ready to respond to fly or bait in the same waters. Then there are other varieties of fish in some of the streams, although none are so numerous as the trout. Salmon run up the Columbia River into the Snake and its many tributaries; there spawn, and return late in the spring or early summer. Sturgeon of enormous size frequently weighing from 600 to 1,000 pounds, are abundant in Snake River. The Payette Lakes and Sawtooth Lakes are the homes of the redfish. This is a large, beautiful fish, weighing from two and a half to six pounds, is of a bright red color (and changing to a beautiful blue soon after being taken from the water), with head and fins of light brown, and is excellent eating. By some they are believed to be the real blue fish of the ocean, whence they come regularly to spawn, like the salmon. A species known as bull trout is found in Payette Lake; they are larger than the ordinary salmon trout, and weigh from five to eleven pounds.

No better trout fishing can be found in the world than in Silver Creek and Wood River, near Hailey, or in the headwaters of Salmon River, Payette River, Snake River, and other streams. Much of the finest fishing is within a stone's throw of the Oregon Short Line Railway.

Grizzly, black, and cinnamon bears are still numerous in the forests and mountains. The silver-tipped bear is more rare. A specimen exhibited at the New Orleans Exposition was captured among the mountains of Sawtooth Range, a few miles north of Ketchum. The American elk is found now chiefly in the northern counties; although a herd of ninety was found by a young hunter from St. Louis, near Hailey, in November, 1888. Antelope are still numerous throughout the Territory, as are also black-tail and white-tail deer.

In addition to those already mentioned, a list of the more common native quadrupeds of the State, would include the Rocky Mountain sheep, California lion, yellow wolf, coyote, moose, wolverine, lynx or catamount, wild cat, fox (black, gray, silver, and cross), weasel, badger, marten, mink, large

striped skunk, small spotted skunk, large gray, ground, pine, and flying
squirrel, chipmunk, otter, raccoon, woodchuck, gopher, mole, wood mouse,
kangaroo rat, and jack rabbit.

The birds are those common to the Northwest. Eagles (bald and golden)
are abundant in the mountains, especially in the neighborhood of streams.
Wild duck, swan, geese, pelican, sage hen, chicken, grouse, and quail are
plentiful in season. The burrowing owl, fish hawk, and buzzard may
be mentioned among the large birds. In addition to these, are the
usual varieties of woodpecker, raven, hawk, pigeon, meadow lark, magpie,
red-winged blackbird, bluebird, robin, snipe, plover, curlew, sparrow, cross
bill, linnet. oriole, California canary, swallow, and two varieties of humming birds.

The huntsman of either large or small game can rendezvous at either
Soda Springs, Pocatello, Hailey, Ketchum, Boise City, Caldwell, Weiser, or
Payette, and not go amiss.

A tourist writing from Hailey recently said: "I have said nothing about
the game we have found in this Territory, and as my letter is already too
long, I will only say that the different varieties supplied by the proprietors
of the Grand Pacific Hotel to their patrons at their world-renowned annual
game dinners could be duplicated here by a couple of hunters in a few days'
time."

## PLEASURE AND HEALTH RESORTS.

Here the "Gem of the Mountains" stands unrivaled. No region of similar
extent on the globe can compare with Idaho in the number, variety, and merit
of attractions for the pleasure and health seeker. The enchanting beauty of
its many Alpine lakes, the majesty and splendor of its thousands of snow-clad
peaks, towering as they do, above the peaceful landscapes of its loveliest
vales, and the indescribable glory of its wondrous cataracts in the depths
of the grandest cañons on earth, enrapture artist and poet alike. Amid
such scenes, what a privilege it is to drink in an atmosphere whose every
breath is a tonic, and to partake of sparkling waters, whose efficacy is
beyond compare. There are other enchanting waters—lakes, rivers, and
rivulets alike—with myriads of trout and other fish disporting themselves
in their translucent depths, or waterfowl covering their often placid sur-
faces, and surrounded by forests inhabited by the elk, bear, deer, mountain sheep, goat, and other game. What a land for the enthusiastic Nimrod
or disciple of Izaak Walton.

The lakes, the rivers, the hunting and fishing, and the all but perfect
climate have already been treated under appropriate headings. As for the
ideal mountain camp grounds, the glades, the parks, and valleys—all mar-
vels of picturesque beauty—they are almost numberless. Various resorts,
where all can spend hours or months of pleasure, already possess the luxu-
ries and conveniences generally supplied by modern hotels elsewhere. The
name of mineral springs—healing waters—is legion. Hot and cold, delicious
as the nectar of the gods, or offensive enough for one's worst enemy, soda,
sulphur, iron, salt, magnesia—these and others of every form known—in

number sufficient for the uses of multitudes and in volume and efficacy apparently ample "for the healing of the nations."

The most remarkable group of mineral springs in America are the Soda Springs of Bingham county, in Eastern Idaho. They are situated in a romantic valley, 5,779 feet above the level of the sea, surrounded by lofty snow-clad mountains, and easily reached from the East or West by the Oregon Short Line, which passes through this region on its way to Portland. Bear River, which is a tributary of Great Salt Lake, flows through this depression in the mountains from east to west. On the north side, Soda Creek, fed by innumerable springs, and carrying a large volume of water, flows down to its junction with Bear River. The town and station of Soda Springs are on this creek, a mile above its junction with Bear River. Within a radius of two or three miles are scores of large springs, the waters ranging from almost ice-cold to warm, containing magnesia, soda, iron, sulphur, and various other constituents, in such proportions as to have a great power on disease, and some of them being so highly charged with carbonic acid and other gases as to prove a most pleasing beverage. The waters are a superb tonic, and are effecting remarkable cures of skin and blood diseases, dyspepsia, rheumatism, and many other ills our flesh is heir to. Steamboat Springs, so named by General Fremont in 1843, have a temperature of 87°. Many of the more prominent springs have names such as the Jewsharp, Hooper, Champagne, Formation, etc., but the one from which water is shipped, and which is free from sediment of all kinds, is called Idanha, the Indian name for Idaho, which means 'Gem of the Mountains." The water from this spring is most palatable, and has a delightfully refreshing and invigorating effect. These delicious soda and magnesia waters are becoming so popular that train-loads are shipped each season to consumers in distant States. The company developing this laudable industry is now able to put up 10,000 bottles daily During a single month in 1888 the Union Pacific Railway shipped over 100 tons of this bottled elixir from Soda Springs Station.

The Soda Springs region abounds in other attractions worth crossing our Continent to see, among them magnificent drives, beautiful lakes, extinct volcanoes, geyser cones, sulphur mountains, a boiling lake of the same material, some wonderful caves, superb fishing and hunting, and an atmosphere calculated to bring the flush of health to any but the most hopeless invalid. It promises to be the great sanitorium of the West, and for years has been the resort of hundreds annually, who have been willing to "stage it" for forty or fifty, or even one hundred miles, to reach its charmed precincts. Soda Creek, Bear River, Blackfoot River, Port Neuf River, and Swan and Bear Lakes are close by, and furnish unlimited numbers of trout The Blackfoot and Port Neuf are particularly the favorite streams for this sport, while in the mountains there are bear and elk.

Says a writer: "Mountain scenery could scarcely be finer than it is here, in this lovely pass through the Wahsatch, and the atmosphere is one of its chief delights. It is dry, cool, and extremely invigorating. One wakes from sleep refreshed, and after a draught from the sparkling Idanha, feels as if he had discovered anew the Fountain of Youth The days are warm, bright, and pleasant, but fires are generally required night and day throughout the summer."

Four miles southwest of Soda Springs is Swan Lake, one of the loveliest natural gems set in the Wahsatch chain. It reclines in an oval basin, whose rim is ten feet above the surrounding country. The shores are densely covered with trees, shrubs, and the luxuriant undergrowth native to that country. The outlet is a series of small, moss-covered basins, symmetrically arranged, the clear water overflowing the banks, trickling into the nearest emerald tub, then successively into others, until it forms a sparkling stream, and dances away to a confluence with Bear River in the valley below. It is a matter of common belief among old residents of the locality that the lake is bottomless, no sounding having yet developed its depth. Adjacent to this fit abode for water nymphs is the singular sulphur lake, out of whose center, liquid sulphur incessantly boils, and coats the shores with thick deposits looking as though it might be the direct out-cropping of Plutonian regions.

The Union Pacific Company has erected a superb hotel at Soda Springs for the accommodation of the thousands of visitors. It is built in the Swiss chalet style, is three stories high, surrounded on three sides by a wide veranda, and surmounted with handsome towers. Is is so built that there are no inside rooms, but from every side one can look out upon the magnificent mountain scenery. It is lighted with electric lights, and has all modern conveniences and comforts, and is kept in the usually faultless style of the Pacific Hotel Company, by whom it has been leased.

Soda Springs is an ideal health resort, to which tens of thousands will journey to find all that could be wished for by the most exacting. Its accessibility; the wildness, singularity, and sublimity of its scenery; the coolness, salubrity, and invigorating influences of its climate, its inviting baths, its veritable founts of youth, its dozens of rivers and lakes, alive with game trout, and its deep solitudes of mountain and forest, only broken as haunts for noble game—these alone would render it a Mecca to be eagerly sought, saying nothing of its other regal charms which could be elaborated in appropriate space.

Westward from Soda Springs, the Oregon Short Line route lies for forty miles amid some of the most interesting, pleasing, and picturesque scenes in all nature. In winding its way down out of the confines of the rugged Wahsatch Mountains to the Great Snake River Valley, it follows Port Neuf River. Giant cones and craters of extinct volcanoes, yawning chasms, extenting into the earth's unknown depths, dark caves, and caverns, lofty palisades, all relics of the volcanic age, vie with the gentler phases of an exquisitely beautiful valley panorama to fill the tourist's eye. The river, sinuous as a serpent's trail, is often broken by loveliest cataracts. The valley is alternately a solid bed of highly-colored wild flowers, a luxuraintly-grassed meadow, and well-tilled fields. Towering supremely into the skies are here and there the snow-capped heights, to complete the realization of an artist's dream. Midway between Soda Springs and Pocatello, a fine group of hot sulphur springs burst from the rocks at the water's edge. Here almost anywhere the angler can land a basket of trout in a few hours within a few feet of the railway track, or the sportsmen can bag his dozen ducks or geese in an equally short period. At Pocatello, where the Oregon Short Line crosses the Utah & Northern Railway, are fine hotel accommodations provided by the Union Pacific Company, and this is an excellent rendezvous for the tourist.

About twenty-five miles west of Pocatello, the Oregon Short Line crosses Snake River amid the roar and spray of the American Falls. It is a wild, weird spectacle, not soon forgotten. Happily for the tourist, nature offered a bold crag in mid river for a pier in just the right location to tempt the constructing engineer—hence the great iron bridge in the very midst of the falls and rapids. While the descent is only about fifty feet, the enormous volume of the river, here spread to some 1,500 feet in width, is so terrifically convulsed by its mad plunge over a variety of elevations, that the beholder is amply repaid by his complete and convenient view from the car-window and platform.

About 100 miles west of American Falls is Shoshone, the point from which the Wood River Branch Railway diverges northward from the main line to the Wood River region. It is also the nearest railway point to the great Shoshone Falls, which are reached by a pleasant twenty-five mile drive southward. Shoshone Falls are Idaho's chief wonder and pride. In some respects they have no equal—and certainly no prototype in the known world. They are the very incarnation of all the intensely fascinating features of the world's few great cataracts. No visitor can say that he has ever elsewhere beheld such a wondrous scene; none will ever regret a trip across our Continent to see it. All are wont to compare Shoshone with Niagara. As well compare two absolutely dissimilar forms of architecture. There is nothing in either to remind one of the other, save the vast basin of foaming, surging waters at the bottom. Niagara winds its way monotonously through a comparatively level country, and drops methodically into a commonplace amphitheatre. It is all power and majesty. Shoshone is this and more. The weirdness and enchantments of its abysmal home, and the singularity and sublimity of its mighty plunge mocks all attempts at description. Shoshone pours torrent-like through one of the grandest cañons on earth. Where it pauses to take its awful leap, particolored and fantastically-wrought cliffs rise straight 1,500 feet above it. All its vast volume is instantly dashed over a myriad of jutting rocks into a world of spray, whose fleecy, graceful columns often ascend 1,000 feet in the air. With somewhat less volume than Niagara, Shoshone is one-third higher, and while its face possesses in the main a regular outline, the minor projections along the line of descent obstruct the downward movement just enough to seemingly transform every atom of water into spray and foam. Here is the indescribable splendor and beauty of Shoshone. It is all activity. Not a moment is the enrapturing scene the same. The gorgeous spray-columns are often dissipated into a thousand fantastic shapes, by coming into contact with glittering masses of snow-white foam, the whole under the radiance of the sun being enhanced to beauty indescribable by the richest colors of the rainbow. The river, within a few rods of the great falls, drops seventy feet, then quickly narrowing to 950 feet in width, the vast volume leaps into an abyss 210 feet deep. Above the brink the whole breadth of the river is broken by a dozen small islands, which the water has curved into fantastic forms; rounding some into low domes, sharpening others into mere pillars, and now and then wearing into deep carves. A luxuriance of ferns and mosses, and almost tropical wealth of green leaves and velvety drapery line the rocks and banks, toning down what would otherwise be an oppressively rugged setting to a picture of rarest beauty. Nature has left little for the hand of art to finish here.

Here is an elegant pen picture by the lamented Richardson: "The cataract is unequaled in the world, save by the Niagara, of which it vividly reminds us. It is not all height like Yosemite, nor all breadth and power like the Great Falls of the Missouri, nor all strength and volume like the Niagara, but combines the three elements. The torrent is less than Niagara, and its crescent summit appears less than 1,000 feet wide. But the descent—210 feet—is one-third greater, while above the brink, solemn portals of lava, rising for hundreds of feet on each bank, supply an element of grandeur which the monarch of cataracts altogether lacks. The fall itself is of the purest white, interspersed with myriads of glittering, glassy drops—a cataract of snow with an avalanche of jewels. Mocking and belittling all human splendor, nature is here in her lace and pearls, her robe of diamonds and tiara of rainbow."

On the south bank of the river, which is reached by ferry, is a well-built and elegantly-furnished hotel, where the tourist will find excellent accommodations. It is located on a beautiful natural lawn 200 feet above, and overlooking the falls. From its balconies can be enjoyed all the finer aspects of the magnificent panorama above faintly outlined. A guide is at hand to point out the many wonders in the immediate vicinity. Among these are the Twin Falls of Snake River, about three miles above the Great Falls. These are 150 feet high and are well worth a visit. Interesting excursions, boating, fishing, and hunting, all are here to invite a summer sojourn. Stages make the trip to and from the railroad in a few hours.

North of Shoshone about fifty miles, the Wood River branch of the Oregon Short Line fairly enters the great Wood River region. Hailey and Ketchum, located in the heart of this region, probably arrive as near to all the requirements of the tourist and health-seeker as any of the resorts of Idaho. They are only twelve miles apart by rail, both picturesquely located on the banks of Wood River, Hailey at an altitude of 5,200 feet, and Ketchum about 500 feet higher.

The tourist who wishes an "outing" where he can enjoy all the advantages of luxurious hotel accommodations and the aids incident to tourist life in one of the prettiest and most progressive little cities in the whole West will be suited at Hailey. Its superb location in the beautiful wood River Valley, in the midst of lofty mountain ranges and on the banks of the swift Wood River, is most attractive. Its delightfully cool, summer climate, and its atmosphere, alone a luxury to breathe, are always restful and invigorating to the visitor from the heated East. Then the bustle, thrift and taste of its 2,500 people, as evidenced by its splendid public buildings and handsome homes, its electric lights, water-works, and other adjuncts to a high civilization, are all conducive to the enjoyment of the health or pleasure seeker.

The Alturas and Merchant's hotels, solid three-story brick structures, with ample accommodations for 150 guests each, are a genuine surprise to all comers. They are elegantly furnished, and the Alturas, whose every apartment is lighted with electricity and whose construction and furnishings were with special regard to the wants of tourists, commands a vista of mountain, river, and valley scenery that is a perpetual delight. The river and several creeks within five minutes' walk are alive with mountain trout. The nearer valleys and hillsides afford good grouse and chicken shooting, while the forests within a day's drive are full of deer and bear. A twelve-mile drive down the beautiful Wood River Valley takes the sportsman to Silver Creek, which is known far and near as the finest trout stream in the western mountains and also affords good duck shooting.

But the crowning glory of this whole region is the famous Hailey Hot Springs, located in full view of the town, and only a mile and a half distant. The ride or walk thither is very pleasant, leading through a picturesque little valley, and the location, in a lovely glen in sight of several rich mines, is very pleasing. Large volumes of water of a temperature of 144°, and containing sulphate of soda, iron, magnesia, sulphur, and other desirable ingredients, are emitted from scores of springs. Four commodious rock-walled and cemented swimming baths, and many solid porcelain tub baths are provided. These are all supplied with elegantly-appointed dressing rooms, lighted by electricity, and under the same roof as the luxuriously-furnished chambers. Many patients have gone to these with chronic cases, believed to be hopeless, of neuralgia, paralysis, dyspepsia, inflammatory or mercurial rheumatism, and other complaints for which the Arkansas springs are considered a specific, and after a few months of bathing and drinking, have left completely restored. The baths are, however, still more popular with those in good health, thousands visiting them annually for the delightfully exhilarating effects of a plunge, and for the many attendant pleasures of this all but perfect resort. The many attractions are thus briefly outlined by a Chicago visitor, of the autumn of 1888, in a letter to his home paper:—

"The Hailey Hot Springs site proves a princely domain, embracing as many natural beauties and advantages for the scheme now unfolding as any between the oceans. To commence with, the hot and cold water from the various groups of springs were piped separately through pipes ranging from four to six inches in diameter down to the most commanding site in full view of, and only one and a half miles from, Hailey, and thence led all through the ample grounds and to the various building sites. This superb water system has used up nearly two miles of pipe, and both hot and cold water have such a gravity pressure that they can be thrown all over the buildings. Then upon foundations broad and deep, was placed the main building, over 100 feet square, with numerous wings and broad verandas, almost entirely encircling it. It is a two-story structure in the old colonial style, most pleasing and appropriate in its setting of lofty mountains and nearer stretches of picturesque valleys. This main building embraces ample restaurant and dining facilities, parlors, reading rooms, billiard rooms for ladies and gentlemen, ten-pin alleys, a grand banqueting and ball room, with a monster old-fashioned fire place in one end, large enough to receive the largest cordwood, etc. It also includes ladies' and gentlemen's dressing and toilet rooms, and numerous solid porcelain baths on both upper and lower floor, and a superb complement of chambers on the second floor, from the windows and balconies, of which can be obtained views which should entrance any one short of a misanthrope. Then, near by, there are ladies' and gents' swimming baths thirty by sixty feet each, of solid masonry, and smoothly cemented with the best Portland cement. These have ample dressing rooms by the dozen, in which the bather can recline in easy chairs or upon comfortable lounges.

"There are other smaller plunge baths for ladies and gentlemen, but what a royal place for a health-giving douche are these large rock-walled, rock-bottomed plunges! There is nothing like them in all the West that I know of, and if they are not quite good enough for the most fastidious bather, think of those snowy porcelain tubs, each with its luxuriously-appointed dressing room. Other features are artistically laid-out grounds, the whole to form a perfect park, with its rippling mountain brooks, placid lakes, and dashing waterfalls, sequestered walks, pleasant drives, ample croquet, lawn tennis, and other amusement grounds—in fact, about everything to coax the visitor to one long summer's pleasure. Hot and cold water is led everywhere in all rooms, even through the commodious barns. The entire establishment is heated with steam. Nor will there be a nook or corner in which the electric light will not gleam forth. Electric annunciators are found in every apartment, even to every dressing room of every bath, and speaking tubes connect the barns, restaurant, and other leading apartments with the office. The company are simply doing what the great merits of the waters, the unsurpassed location, the all but perfect climate, the superb trout fishing and hunting, magnificent scenery, and the miles of the finest natural drives to be found in any mountain country on earth, fully justify. These springs, with the rudest appliances, have worked wonderful cures upon hundreds who have come afflicted with rheumatism, dyspepsia, lead poisoning, liver and kidney troubles, and various disorders of the blood. With all these splendid facilities for their use, they will now soon be the resort of tens of thousands.

Bolton's Hot Springs, located on Deer Creek, five miles from Hailey, are also a strong attraction. Their waters, which are led into well-arranged tub and plunge baths, are efficacious for all blood diseases. The drive thither, the fishing within a stone's throw, the boating and hunting, are all features worthy of note.

Ketchum also combines many attractions for the summer visitor. There is choice of several streams affording superb trout fishing. Pleasant drives lead into surrounding mountains in all directions, and the summer climate is all that could be desired. The Guyer Hot Springs, however, are the great attraction at Ketchum. They are located in a most romantic nook about two miles from Ketchum, on the banks of Warm Springs Creek. An immense volume of water here bursts from many crevices in the rocks, at a temperature of about 150°, and where not confined, drops in many pretty falls into the creek, some twenty feet below. These springs are especially applicable to the cure of rheumatism, and the long train of diseases led by or intimately associated with dyspepsia, gout, liver complaints, and impurities of the blood. Patients suffering with such disorders often derive about as much benefit from drinking the waters as from bathing in them. Among the improvements are a two-story hotel, in which Brussels carpets and nice, soft beds are leading features, with reception and dining hall, billiard halls, extenive stables, cottages for guests, two large plunge baths, a number of tub baths, etc. The water is conveyed through pipes from the springs to the several bath houses, and is so arranged that any desired temperature can be had. Some neatly furnished sleeping rooms have baths attached, so that patients who desire can have all the benefits without any exposure to the outer air, or without necessitating leaving their room. The cuisine and all details of entertainment are home-like and excellent. Following is an analysis of the Guyer Spring water, made by Prof. R. Ogden Doremus, of Bellevue Hospital Medical College, New York:—

|                                               | Grains per Imp. gal. |
|-----------------------------------------------|----------------------|
| Sodium Chloride                               | 3.578                |
| Sodium Carbonate                              | 9.965                |
| Calcium Sulphate                              | 6.574                |
| Magnesium, Sulphate                           | 0.534                |
| Magnesium, Chloride                           | 0.914                |
| Organic Matter, with traces of Iron and Silica| 1.240                |
| Total Solids                                  | 22.805               |

North of Ketchum twenty-five miles is the wonderfully rugged Saw-tooth region, so named on account of the abruptness of the mountain range, which is its central figure. It is the ideal " camping out " corner of Idaho. Hundreds yearly avail themselves of its surpassing attractions in the way of enchanting lakes, towering snow-capped mountains, trout streams, and hot springs. The trip from either Hailey or Ketchum is one of continued delight, and everything in the way of an outfit can be procured at either place. An exhilarating atmosphere and healing waters, in the midst of noble pines and enchanting scenery, fishing, hunting, riding, and exploring, and excellent hotel accommodations, an ever-fruitful field for the mind in the mining, milling, and railway enterprises—these, together with an easy accessibility, are a few of the attributes which in the future will render Hailey and Ketchum the most popular of Rocky Mountain resorts.

Among the attractions of Western Idaho are the Boise Hot Springs, four miles east of Boise City. The springs are highly medicinal, containing iron, sulphur, soda, lime, and magnesia. There are vapor, shower, plunge, and mud baths. The temperature of the springs varies from 125° to 220° Fahrenheit. They are already favorite resorts, and need only to be known to become widely celebrated.

Tourists will be interested in the fact that Idaho possesses about 600,000 acres of lake area. Scattered among the mountain ranges are countless lakes of every destription. Kootenai is the lake county of Idaho. Within her boundaries are Cœur d'Alene, Pend d'Oreille, Kaniskú, Cocolalla, and numerous smaller lakes. Cœur d'Alene Lake is about thirty miles long, with a width varying from two to four miles. A daily line of steamers plies its waters from Cœur d'Alene, to the Old Mission. Its waters are clear and cool, and abound in fish. The banks are mountainous, covered with timber, Cœur d'Alene, St. Joseph and St. Mary's Rivers flow into it, and the Spokane is its outlet. At the lower end of the lake a commodious hotel offers accommodations for visitors and tourists.

Lake Pend d'Oreille is doubtless one of the most beautiful sheets of water in the United States. It is of irregular shape, about sixty miles in length, and of a width varying from three to fifteen miles. It is in reality a widening of Clark's Fork, and winds its picturesque way among the wood-covered mountains, which rise up from its shores in a never-ceasing panorama of beautiful surprise. There are two steamers on the lake at present. If unsurpassed natural scenery, abundance of fish, and plenty of game in the surrounding forests can offer any attractions, Pend d'Oreille must, within a few years, become one of the most noted resorts in the Northwest.

Kanisku Lake, in the northern part of the county, is about twenty miles long, and half as wide. This and others are situated in wild and still unexplored regions. Lake Waha is a favorite resort for the people at Lewiston. It is a small sheet of water not two miles long, and about half a mile wide. Its banks are precipitous, and covered with timber. One of its chief claims to popularity is its abundance of trout. An enthusiastic writer, in referring to Waha, says: "Nothing we have ever seen can exceed the tranquil beauty of this sylvan, this idyllic scene, with its mountain solitudes, unbroken by a discordant sound, and its wealth of charming landscape and xanthic skies."

Payette Lake is one of the sources of Payette River. It is situated in Boise county, about eighty-five miles north of Caldwell, on the Oregon Short Line, and is rapidly becoming a favorite resort for the people of Southern Idaho. It is about ten miles long and about half as wide. It is surrounded by mountains and is famous for its trout, red fish, and white fish. Its depth is unknown.

Among the most beautiful of the smaller lakes is Tahoma, situated in the Sawtooth Mountains at an elevation of 8,000 feet. It is about forty miles north of Ketchum, the present terminus of the Wood River Branch of the Oregon Short line, and is reached by one of the most picturesque mountain roads in the world. Twenty miles distant is the Lower or Big Sawtooth Lake. With the exception of the narrow, level space traversed by the road, the lake is mountain-locked, the peaks on one side rising a thousand feet above the surface of the water. These peaks are covered with evergreen timber, such as pine, spruce, and fir, while on the other side a mass of granite crags rises 1,500 feet. From one of these crags leaps a large mountain stream, forming a fall some five hundred feet high, and completing one of the most exquisitely beautiful pictures in all nature. The lake is three by nine miles in extent, and has been sounded to a depth of 1,000 feet without striking bottom.

Bear Lake lies in Southeastern Idaho and Northern Utah, the dividing line running through the center of the lake east and west, and is about twenty miles long and eight miles wide. It abounds in fish of various kinds, such as several kinds of trout—viz.: salmon trout, silver trout, speckled trout, and mountain brook trout, also mullet and white fish, as well as chubs. The lake is fed by several mountain streams, and these also abound in fish. It has an outlet emptying into Bear River in the north. The shores of the lake are sandy and gravelly, affording a clean and easy approach. The water is shallow for a distance of about a hundred yards, when it gradually deepens to an extent not as yet determined. The water is very clear, affording a view of the bottom at a depth of ten to fifteen feet. It is a splendid bathing resort, and the inhabitants living on its shores delight in this exercise, as well as others who visit the lake in the summer from distant localities. The Oregon Short Line skirts the northern shore. No doubt can exist in the mind of anyone who has visited this beautiful lake, but in the near future this will be a favorite summer resort for the sportsman, the tourist and the pleasure-seeker, and that good hotels and accommodations will be provided, and the lake decked with sails.

Henry Lake, about forty miles east of the Utah & Northern Railway, on the Union Pacific route to Yellowstone National Park, is the admiration of all visitors. Its altitude is 6,443 feet, and it is two miles wide by five miles long. Peaks of the Rocky Mountains rise majestically 3,000 feet from near its shores. Its surface is dotted with islands and indented with graceful tongues of land, rich in foliage. Near by is Cliff Lake, which is three miles long by half a mile wide, and in whose azure depth 1,400 feet of line has failed to reach bottom. It is almost surrounded by vertical basaltic cliffs, while a conical pine-covered island rises from its bosom. Henry Lake and surroundings are well worthy a two or three days' halt, by those who delight in mountaineering, hunting, fishing, and sailing, or desire rest.

Sixteen miles south of Caldwell, on the banks of Snake River, are the Given Hot Springs, which have effected some marvelous cures of rheumatism and kindred diseases. North of Caldwell from fifty to one hundred miles, and the great summer camping-grounds of the residents of Western Idaho. These are along Payette River, at Payette Lakes (already described), and in Salmon Meadows—a mountain park deservedly famous for its magnificent scenery, its superb climate, its rivers and creeks full of trout, and its mountain ranges alive with noble game. All these can be reached by easy drives from Caldwell and Weiser, on the Oregon Short Line.

These are only a few of the Idaho resorts. Her hundreds of others from one to two miles above sea-level afford an atmosphere which is an elixir itself. Into her princely area of 55,228,160 acres are crowded every variety of valley and mountain temperature. Sunshine, dry streets and a maximum of warm days may be enjoyed in her sheltered valleys in winter, or flowers and snow-banks and a frosty atmosphere may garnish the mountain camp-ground in midsummer. The range of mineral waters for either bathing or drinking purposes is greater than in any region of similar extent on the globe. Hot sulphur and soda for bathing, cold soda, seltzer, iron, chalybeate and sulphur for drinking, are found at altitudes ranging from 2,000 to 8,000 feet above the sea, and in numerous cases are within sight of the railway. The scenic attractions are none the less varied. The invalid, whose mind *must* feed on something, can combine business and profit with the great aim of his sojourn, for adjacent to the most charming health-resorts are Idaho's grandest mining, smelting, and railroad enterprises. These offer an ever fruitful study, and always present a field for business venture. Life everywhere is safe, and travel easy. No region of such multiplied attractions could be more accessible than this has now been rendered by the Union Pacific Railway. These unparalleled attractions have already made the State the resort of thousands of summer visitors in search of health and recreation, and the permanent home of thousands of others who have fled from unhealthful sections of the East. When the remarkable cures which have been effected by these combined agencies are better known and understood, when Idaho becomes less of a *terra incognita* to the teeming populations of the East, then it will be felt that no extravagant claim is being made for the State when it is called the "Great Sanitarium of the United States."

## BUSINESS OPENINGS.

Money commands from 12 to 18 per cent per annum; Idaho affords fine opportunities for business men of either large or limited means, who will be content with profits ranging from 15 to 25 per cent interest on capital invested. Capital, directed by sagacity and enterprise, possesses great advantages here as elsewhere; indeed, the new avenues being continually opened by the rapid development of a beautiful new country, multiply the opportunities for its profitable employment. There is scarcely any reputable vocation wherein the same capital and good management which insures success in Eastern communities will not yield greater returns here. Now, above all other periods, is the time to put money into commercial ventures, real estate, mines, or live stock, as the heavy immigration will enhance the value of such property to a degree not now possible to comprehend. It is unnecessary for anyone to load himself down with the common necessaries of life, and transport them to such a region as Idaho. Outfitting houses of every nature, with such immense stocks of goods as are rarely found in cities of 20,000 inhabitants in the East, are found in the various towns of Idaho. The shipments made by these firms are so large and judiciously handled that no individual can afford to bring articles of ordinary use from distant States.

## IDAHO'S AGRICULTURE.

A gentleman writes us to inquire if we make any claims for Idaho as an agricultural State. Most certainly we do. Though she has vast mineral resources, we believe that Idaho will be known pre-eminently as an agricultural State. Agriculture is in its infancy here, yet this year's crops are reported as follows: Wheat, 3,469,300 bushels; oats, 2,140,860 bushels; barley, 1,150,450 bushels; corn, 407,400 bushels; rye, 640,900 bushels; grass seeds, 17,350 pounds; hay, 424,740 tons; potatoes, 1,850,900, bushels; other vegetables, 838,000 bushels; apples, 277,000 bushels; pears, 29,850 boxes; peaches, 34,850 boxes; plums and prunes, 34,350 boxes; grapes, 18,200 boxes; berries of all kinds, 76,600 boxes.

Live stock returned for assessment, which undoubtedly is much less than the true number: Thoroughbred horses, 1,113; graded horses, 21,428; native horses, 105,263; mules, 2,480; jacks and jennies, 206; thoroughbred bulls, 1,400; thoroughbred cows, 1,440; graded bulls, 4,322; graded cows, 21,067; range cattle, 350,225; work oxen, 1,422; imported sheep, 3,120; graded sheep, 65,500; common sheep, 317,274; Angora goats, 5,565; hogs, 38,074. Is not all this a pretty good showing as an agricultural State in its infancy?

For agricultural purposes there is no finer climate on the globe than that found in Idaho—and the same may be said of its soil. In Northern Idaho rains are frequent, and there is no resort to irrigation, which is necessary in Southern Idaho. Apples, pears, plums and prunes, both in quantity and quality, flourish in Idaho as in the most favored spots of the world. The amount of fruit raised per acre would seem fabulous in its statement to any one not familiar with the orchards of this young State. One thousand bushels per acre is not an unusual average of the apple crop. The average grain crops can be stated at these figures: Wheat, forty bushels to the acre, and in some seasons the average is as high as sixty bushels; oats will average from sixty-five to seventy bushels to the acre; barley will average from forty-five to fifty bushels to the acre. Corn is not a first-class crop in Idaho. Potatoes, from 200 to 500 bushels per acre, and sometimes a thousand bushels to the acre; onions, the same as potatoes; hay, from four to seven tons per acre—an average probably would be a little more than five tons; of timothy, clover and alfalfa, there are two crops in Idaho, and sometimes three.

The abundant pasturage, the great crops of hay, and her mild winters, make Idaho an exceptionally fine country for stock raising. So as an agricultural country, we know of no section of the Union, taking it all in all, that is the equal of Idaho. When a stranger is asked to consider our large crops, he should remember that Idaho, in distant ages, has been subjected to great volcanic overflow, which in the process of disintegration has left in the soil rich supplies of salts and minerals which are the luxuriant support of plant and vegetable life.—*Boise Statesman.*

## IDAHO ALTITUDES.

Elevations of prominent towns, lakes, valleys, etc:—

| NAME. | Eleva-tion. | NAME | Eleva-tion. |
|---|---|---|---|
| | *Feet.* | | *Feet.* |
| Albion | 4,400 | Long Valley | 3,700 |
| Alturas Lake | 6,600 | Murray | 2,750 |
| American Falls | 4,320 | Malad City | 4,700 |
| Atlanta | 5,525 | Market Lake | 4,795 |
| Bear Lake | 5,900 | Montpelier | 5,793 |
| Bellevue | 5,200 | Mouth of Port Neuf River | 4,522 |
| Blackfoot City | 4,523 | Mount Idaho City | 3,480 |
| Bloomington | 5,985 | Montana Mine | 9,500 |
| Boise City, capital of Idaho | 2,800 | Meade Mountain | 10,540 |
| Big Camas Prairie, Alturas County | 5,000 | Malad Divide | 9,220 |
| Big Camas Prairie, Idaho County | 3,500 | Oneida Salt Works | 6,300 |
| Bonanza City | 6,400 | Oneida (town) | 5,700 |
| Burke | 3,900 | Oxford | 4,862 |
| Camas Station | 4,722 | Paris | 5,836 |
| Cœur d'Alene Mission | 2,280 | Pocatello | 4,512 |
| Craig Mountain | 4,080 | Paris Peak | 9,522 |
| Custer Mountain | 8,760 | Placerville | 5,100 |
| Caribou Mountain | 9,854 | Putnam Mountain | 8,983 |
| Centerville | 4,825 | Quartzburg | 5,115 |
| Challis | 5,400 | Rathdrum | 2,000 |
| Clawson Toll Gate | 4,300 | Ross Fork Station | 4,894 |
| Custer City | 6,560 | Red Rock Ranch | 4,792 |
| Dry Creek Station | 5,689 | Rock Creek | 4,513 |
| Eagle Rock | 4,720 | Rocky Bar | 5,200 |
| Estes Mountain | 10,050 | Red Fish Lake | 6,600 |
| Fort Hall | 4,788 | Sawtell's Peak | 9,070 |
| Fort Lapwai | 2,000 | St. Charles | 5,932 |
| Franklin City | 4,516 | St. George | 5,771 |
| Florida Mountain | 7,750 | Salmon City | 4,080 |
| Florence | 8,000 | Soda Springs | 5,779 |
| Fish Haven | 5,932 | Silver City | 6,680 |
| Forks of Lolo | 4,450 | Sawtooth City | 7,000 |
| Gentile Valley (head) | 5,245 | Shoshone | 4,587 |
| Galena City | 7,900 | Summit, between Challis and Bo- | |
| Gladiator Mine | 9,700 |   nanza | 9,100 |
| Henry Lake | 6,443 | Summit, between Boise City and | |
| Hailey | 5,850 |   Idaho | 4,815 |
| Idaho City | 4,263 | Summit, between Idaho City and | |
| Junction Station | 6,329 |   Centerville | 4,812 |
| Jackson Lake | 6,806 | South Mountain City | 6,450 |
| Ketchum | 5,700 | Salmon Falls | 3,226 |
| Lewiston | 680 | War Eagle Mountain | 7,980 |
| Lake Pend d'Oreille | 2,003 | Weston | 4,600 |
| Lake Cœur d'Alene | 2,150 | Weiser City | 2,340 |

# WILL TELL YOU ALL ABOUT IT.

Any Ticket Agent in the United States or Canada can sell Tickets, check Baggage, and arrange
or Pullman Palace Sleeping Car berths, via the Union Pacific Railway.
Do not complete your arrangements for a Western trip until you have
applied to the undersigned. Additional information, Maps,
Time Tables, etc., will be cheerfully furnished.

**BOSTON, MASS.**—290 Washington St.—W. S.
CONDELL, New England Freight and Pas-
senger Agent.
E. M. NEWBEGIN, Traveling Freight and
Passenger Agent.

**BUTTE, MONT.**—Cor. Main and Broadway.—
E. V. MAZE, General Agent.

**CHATTANOOGA, TENN.**—P. O. Box, 543.—
F. L. LYNDE, Traveling Passenger Agent.

**CHEYENNE, WYO.**—C. W. SWEET, Freight and
Ticket Agent.

**CHICAGO, ILL.**—191 S. Clark St.—W. H. KNIGHT,
Gen'l Agent Freight and Passenger Dep'ts.
T. W. YOUNG, Traveling Passenger Agent.
D. W. JOHNSTON, Traveling Passenger Agent.
W. T. HOLLY, City Passenger Agent.

**CINCINNATI, OHIO.**—27 West Fourth St.—J. D.
WELSH, General Agent Freight and Pas-
senger Departments.
A. G. SHEARMAN, Traveling Freight and Pas-
senger Agent.
T. C. HIRST, Traveling Passenger Agent.

**COUNCIL BLUFFS, IOWA.**—
A. J. MANDERSON, Gen'l Agent, U.P.Transfer.
R. W. CHAMBERLAIN, Passenger Agent.
J. W. MAYNARD, Ticket Agent.
J. C. MITCHELL, City Ticket Agent.

**DENVER, COL.**—1708 Larimer St.—GEO. ADY,
General Agent.
C. H. TITUS, Traveling Passenger Agent.
E. G. PATTERSON, City Ticket Agent.
F. G. ERB, City Passenger Agent.
E. F. LACKNER, Ticket Agent, Union Depot.

**DES MOINES, IOWA.**—218 Fourth St.—E. M.
FORD, Traveling Passenger Agent.

**FT. WORTH, TEX.**—D. B. KEELER, General
Freight & Pass. Agent, Ft. Worth & D. C. Ry.
A. J. RATCLIFFE, Traveling Passenger Agent.
N. S. DAVIS, City Ticket Agent, 401 Main
Street.

**HELENA, MONT.**—28 North Main St.—H. O.
WILSON, Freight and Passenger Agent.

**KANSAS CITY, MO.**—1038 Union Ave.—J. B.
FRAWLEY, General Agent.
J. B. REESE, Traveling Passenger Agent.
H. K. PROUDFIT, City Passenger Agent.
T. A. SHAW, Ticket Agent.
C. A. WHITTIER, City Ticket Agent.
A. W. MILLSPAUGH, Ticket Ag't, Union Depot.

**LONDON, ENGLAND**—Ludgate Circus.—THOS.
COOK & SON, European Passenger Agents.

**LOS ANGELES, CAL.**—229 South Spring St.—
G. F. HERR, Passenger Agent.

**NEW WHATCOM, WASH.**—J. W. ALTON, Gen'l
Agent Freight and Passenger Departments.

**NEW YORK CITY.**—287 Broadway.—R. TEN-
BROECK, General Eastern Agent.
J. D. TENBROECK, Traveling Passenger Agent.
S. A. HUTCHISON, Traveling Passenger Agent.
WM. A. DOLAN, Traveling Passenger Agent.
J. F. WILEY, City Passenger Agent.

**OAKLAND, CAL.**—Twelfth and Broadway.—
GEO. B. SEAMAN, Passenger Agent.

**OGDEN, UTAH.**—Union Depot.—C. A. HENRY,
Ticket Agent.

**OLYMPIA, WASH.**—Percival's Wharf.—J. C.
PERCIVAL, Ticket Agent.

**OMAHA, NEB.**—1302 Farnam St.—HARRY P.
DEUEL, City Ticket Agent.
FRANK N. PROPHET, City Passenger Agent.
M. J. GREEVY, Traveling Passenger Agent,
9th and Farnam streets.
J. K. CHAMBERS, Ticket Agent, Union Depot.

**PITTSBURGH, PA.**—400 Wood St.—S. C. MIL-
BOURNE, Traveling Passenger Agent.

**PORTLAND, ORE.**—54 Washington St.—W. H.
HURLBURT, Assistant General Pass'r Agent.
GEO. H. HILL, Traveling Passenger Agent.
V. A. SCHILLING, City Ticket Agent.
A. J. GOODRICH, City Passenger Agent.
A. L. MAXWELL, Ticket Ag't. Grd. Cent'l Stat.

**PORT ANGELES, WASH.**—R. R. HARDING, Agt.

**PORT TOWNSEND, WASH.**—Union Wharf.—
H. R. TIBBALS, Ticket Agent.

**PUEBLO, COL.**—233 North Union Ave.—A. S.
CUTHBERTSON, General Agent.

**ST. JOSEPH, MO.**—Chamber of Commerce.—
S. M. ADSIT, General Freight and Passenger
Agent, St. J. & G. I. R. R.
F. P. WADE, City Ticket Agent, Corner 3d
and Francis Sts.
Jo. HANSON, Ticket Agent, Union Depot.

**ST. LOUIS, MO.**—213 N. 4th St.—J. F. AGLAR.
Gen'l Agent Freight and Pass. Departments.
N. HAIGHT, Traveling Passenger Agent.
E. R. TUTTLE, Traveling Passenger Agent.
E. A. WILLIAMS, City Fr't and Passenger Agt.

**SALT LAKE CITY, UTAH.**—201 Main St.—D. E.
BURLEY, General Agent.
D. S. TAGGART, Traveling Passenger Agent.
C. P. CANFIELD, Traveling Passenger Agent.
F. F. ECCLES, City Ticket Agent.
W. S. EVANS, City Passenger Agent.

**SAN FRANCISCO, CAL.**—1 Montgomery St.—
D. W. HITCHCOCK, General Agent.
MALONE JOYCE, Traveling Passenger Agent.
W. R. VICE, Pacific Coast Passenger Agent.
J. F. FUGAZI, Emig. Ag't, 19 Montgomery Ave.

**SEATTLE, WASH.**—705 Second St.—A. C. MAR-
TIN, General Agent.

**SIOUX CITY, IOWA.**—503 Fourth St.—D. M.
COLLINS, General Agent.
GEO. E. ABBOTT, Tr'g Fr't and Pass'r Agent.
H. H. BIRDSALL, City Ticket Agent.
GEO. LEDYARD, City Passenger Agent.
GEO. E. WHEELOCK, Ticket Ag't, Union Depot.

**SPOKANE, WASH.**—Cor. Riverside and Washington.—PERRY GRIFFIN, P. and Tkt. Agt.

**TACOMA, WASH.**—903 Pacific Ave.—E. E. ELLIS,
General Agent.

**TRINIDAD, COL.**—J. F. LINTHURST, Tkt. Agt.

**VICTORIA, B. C.**—100 Government St.—C. G.
RAWLINS, Ticket Agent.

---

**E. L. LOMAX,**
General Passenger and Ticket Agent,

**J. N. BROWN,**
Acting Assistant Gen'l Pass'r and Ticket Agent,

# OMAHA, NEB.

www.ingramcontent.com/pod-product-compliance
Lightning Source LLC
Chambersburg PA
CBHW031439280326
41927CB00038B/1127